11/09

100 THINGS
COWBOYS FANS
SHOULD KNOW & DO
BEFORE THEY DIE

Ed Housewright

TRIUMPH
BOOKS

Grand County Public Library
Moab, Utah 84532

Copyright © 2008 by Ed Housewright

No part of this publication may be reproduced, stored in a retrieval system, or transmitted in any form by any means, electronic, mechanical, photocopying, or otherwise, without the prior written permission of the publisher, Triumph Books, 542 South Dearborn Street, Suite 750, Chicago, Illinois 60605.

Triumph Books and colophon are registered trademarks of Random House, Inc.

Library of Congress Cataloging-in-Publication Data

Housewright, Ed.
100 things Cowboys fans should know & do before they die / Ed Housewright.
   p. cm.
   Includes bibliographical references.
   ISBN-13: 978-1-60078-080-6
   ISBN-10: 1-60078-080-6
   1. Dallas Cowboys (Football team) 2. Dallas Cowboys (Football team)—Miscellanea. I. Title.
      GV956.D3H67 2008
      796.332'6407642812—dc22
                              2008021508

This book is available in quantity at special discounts for your group or organization. For further information, contact:
   Triumph Books
   542 South Dearborn Street
   Suite 750
   Chicago, Illinois 60605
   (312) 939–3330
   Fax (312) 663–3557

Printed in U.S.A.
ISBN: 978-1-60078-080-6
Content packaged by Mojo Media, Inc.
Joe Funk: Editor
Jason Hinman: Creative Director
All photos courtesy of AP Images except where otherwise noted.

To my wife, Gwen, and son, Connor. Thanks for your undying patience, love, and support.

Contents

Foreword

I never expected to get to play for the Dallas Cowboys.

Coming out of college in 1977 I knew I would be a top draft pick. However, I faced a dilemma. The two-year-old Seattle Seahawks, one of the worst teams in the NFL, wanted to draft me, but I didn't want to play in Seattle.

Even the best running backs need a good offensive line, and the Seahawks didn't have one. I weighed only 185 pounds; that meant some defensive linemen would outweigh me by 100 pounds. If they unloaded on me week after week, "TD" wouldn't have a very productive NFL career.

My agent and I started dropping hints that I wouldn't play in Seattle if they drafted me. I said I'd head north of the border and play in the Canadian Football League. I was bluffing, but the strategy worked. The Seahawks, nervous that they'd waste their top draft, started looking for a trade.

The Cowboys, thank the Lord, needed a running back and wanted to deal. They swapped four future draft picks to Seattle for the right to draft me. I couldn't believe my good fortune! Instantly, I went from the league's doghouse to the penthouse.

In my rookie year, we won the Super Bowl, beating the Denver Broncos, 27–10. How's that for starting a career? In my 11 seasons with the Cowboys I rushed for 12,036 yards and scored 72 rushing touchdowns. I played my final season in Denver, but I'll always be a Cowboy.

Today, I'm very fortunate to be in the Pro Football Hall of Fame, and I'm grateful to the Dallas Cowboys for helping me achieve my individual and team goals. I have nothing but fond memories from my years with the Cowboys. Coach Landry could be demanding, but he taught me valuable lessons that made me a better football player and person.

My teammates and I were blessed to play for a team that epitomized class and an unwavering commitment to winning. The Cowboys truly are "America's Team." As you read this book, you'll understand our pride in being part of the Cowboys legacy.

And you'll understand the devotion of diehard Cowboys fans around the country.

— **Tony Dorsett**

Introduction

The Dallas Cowboys are America's Team. Okay, the nickname is a cliché. It sounds presumptuous, but it's true. The Cowboys have a national following like no other NFL team. Fans cheer the Cowboys from coast to coast and border to border. They even have an international following. The Cowboys have drawn huge crowds when they've played exhibition games in England and Mexico. Their games are regularly broadcast in Spanish, and Mexican citizens travel north to attend home games.

Why do the Cowboys have such appeal? First, they have an incredible winning tradition. The Cowboys have appeared in eight Super Bowls, more than any other team, and they tie with Pittsburgh and San Francisco for having the most wins—five. From the mid-1960s to mid-1980s, the Cowboys compiled 20 consecutive winning seasons. No other team has ever matched that consistency.

Second, the Cowboys attract flashy, high-profile players. The current roster includes Terrell Owens, a loud-mouthed but exceptionally talented wide receiver, and Tony Romo, who has the best rags-to-riches story in the NFL. Romo joined the Cowboys five years ago as a free agent, and is now an All-Pro quarterback. Owens and Romo join Deion Sanders, Emmitt Smith, Troy Aikman, Michael Irvin, Tony Dorsett, Roger Staubach, and many other Cowboys who have captivated the country with their talent and charisma.

Third, the Cowboys organization, intentionally or unintentionally, creates a soap-opera-like atmosphere that's hard to ignore. Owner Jerry Jones bought the team almost two decades ago, and immediately fired beloved coach Tom Landry. He brought in brash college coach Jimmy Johnson, who magically transformed the Cowboys from losers to two-time Super Bowl champs. Then Johnson quit and Jones brought in another college coach, Barry Switzer. He, too, won a Super Bowl before stepping down. Two coaches later, Jones tapped Bill Parcells, the biggest name in NFL coaching.

Jones thrives on publicity. He's receiving plenty for building an unrivaled, $1 billion stadium, set to open in 2009. Super Bowl XLV is to be played there in 2011.

This book, *100 Things Cowboys Fans Should Know & Do Before They Die*, starts by listing the greatest Cowboy of all time. Care to guess? Read the first item and see if you were right. The book then lists, in descending order, the next 99 most important facts to know or activities to do.

The things-to-know items include an overview of the classic Ice Bowl, a recap of the troubled life of star linebacker Thomas "Hollywood" Henderson, and a discussion of the Cowboys' 52–17 rout of Buffalo in Super Bowl XXVII.

The things-to-do items start with visiting Texas Stadium (before the Cowboys move to the new stadium) and walking through the Don Meredith Museum in the quarterback's hometown of Mount Vernon, Texas.

As the Cowboys near their 50th birthday, they are more popular than ever. In 2007 they compiled a 13–3 record and sent a league-high 13 players to the Pro Bowl. Everyone expected the Cowboys to face the undefeated New England Patriots in Super Bowl XLII. Instead, the Cowboys lost to a wild-card team they'd beaten twice: the New York Giants. The upset thrust the Cowboys further into the spotlight. Even in losing, they demanded attention.

The Cowboys' early exit in 2007 will generate even more interest for the 2008 season. Will Owens keep quiet and have another banner year? Or will he grow discontent, as he has with other teams, and become a distraction? Will Romo set more Cowboys' passing records, or will his fairytale story come to an end?

Stay tuned. The Cowboys are the most talented, entertaining team in the league. They're more fun to watch than any reality show on television.

1 Roger Staubach

Roger Staubach is the all-time greatest Dallas Cowboy.

Disagree? Okay, let's look at some of the other contenders.

Maybe you'd nominate Emmitt Smith, the National Football League's all-time leading rusher and an integral part of the Cowboys' three 1990s Super Bowl wins. You could make a case for defensive lineman Bob Lilly, the Cowboys' first-ever draft choice and one of the best in NFL history. Michael Irvin, the Cowboys' all-time leading receiver, and another cog in the Super Bowl wins of the '90s, deserves consideration. So does quarterback Troy Aikman. After all, Aikman won more Super Bowls than Staubach (three to two), had more completions (2,898 to 1,685), and threw more touchdown passes (165 to 153). All are great players. All are in the Hall of Fame, except for Smith, who will be soon.

But neither they, nor anyone else in the Cowboys' 48-year history, can match Staubach's intensity, leadership, and flair for the dramatic. Staubach engineered 23 fourth-quarter comebacks to win games, including 14 in the final two minutes or overtime. He beat opponents with his elusive scrambling and pinpoint passing.

"He was the epitome of a competitor, the leader of leaders," said Cowboys defensive back Charlie Waters.

Staubach's heroics on the field, combined with his clean living off the field, made him an icon in Dallas. He helped create the image of the Cowboys as America's Team.

Staubach's story is enhanced by his uphill journey to success. He didn't take his first NFL snap until he was 27 years old. After graduating from the U.S. Naval Academy, where he won the Heisman Trophy, Staubach had to fulfill a four-year military commitment. As a result, teams shied away from him in the 1964 draft. The Cowboys invested only a 10th-round pick in him, but Staubach quickly showed his desire to succeed in the NFL. He stayed in tiptop shape while in the service, quarterbacked a Navy base team,

Roger Staubach looks for an open receiver during Super Bowl X on January 18, 1976, in Miami against the Pittsburgh Steelers.

and practiced with footballs mailed to him by the Cowboys. Staubach studied the playbook and worked out with the team during training camp.

When he finally joined the Cowboys in July 1969, he wasn't guaranteed to make the team, much less become the starter. Craig Morton seemed to be the quarterback of the future. Morton had spent four years as a capable backup to Don Meredith, who had retired just as Staubach was arriving.

Staubach impressed the coaches early on, but Morton, as expected, won the starting job. In his rookie season, Staubach threw only 47 passes, completing 23, and throwing one touchdown. In his second year, he played more, completing 44 of 82 passes with two touchdowns. By 1971, Staubach had won coach Tom Landry's confidence. Landry began the season alternating Staubach and Morton as starters. But with a 4–3 record at the midpoint, Landry made a move that forever changed the franchise's direction. He named Staubach the lone starter.

In his first game, he led the Cowboys to a come-from-behind win—a fitting omen for the future. Staubach completed 20 of 31 passes, and the Cowboys defeated the St. Louis Cardinals, 16–13. The Staubach-led Cowboys won the remaining six games. He completed almost 60 percent of his passes during the season, throwing 15 touchdowns and only four interceptions.

In the playoffs, Staubach guided the Cowboys to two straight playoff wins, and a berth in Super Bowl VI. He capped his magical season with a 24–3 drubbing of the Miami Dolphins. Staubach threw two touchdown passes and took home the Most Valuable Player award.

The Staubach legend was born.

2 First Season

In their first season in 1960, the Cowboys were abysmal. They finished 0–11–1 and gave no indication of the successful decades yet to come. The Cowboys lost by scores of 48–7, 45–7, and 41–7. Teams

Lousy Facilities

Today, the Cowboys have some of the NFL's best practice facilities. In 1960, they had the worst. The Cowboys practiced at Burnett Field, an abandoned minor league baseball park. The field flooded when it rained, forcing the team to practice at city parks. The locker room showers rarely had hot water, rats chewed on the players' equipment at night, and holes in the walls made it impossible to heat the dressing area. Players once set a barrel of trash on fire to stay warm.

The Cowboys practiced at Burnett Field for two seasons before moving to new digs in North Dallas. Finally, they had facilities befitting an NFL team.

pummeled them week after week.

The season's highlight was a 31–31 tie against the New York Giants, the team Tom Landry left to coach the Cowboys. He had been the Giants' defensive coordinator, and his knowledge of the Giants helped account for the unexpected outcome.

The Cowboys had no stars and few good players the first year. Eddie LeBaron, known as "Little Eddie" because of his 5' 7" stature, quarterbacked the team. He had recently retired from a respectable career with the Washington Redskins, and the Cowboys persuaded him to come back and lead the expansion team.

Dallas didn't have the benefit of a college draft in 1960 to fill the roster with young talent. Instead, the league's 12 other teams each made three players available for selection. With a few exceptions, such as linebacker Jerry Tubbs and receiver Frank Clarke, most of the Cowboys' picks were over-the-hill veterans or unprepared young players.

Dallas residents greeted the new team with apathy. The largest crowd was 30,000—less than half the 75,000-seat capacity of the Cotton Bowl. The last home game drew only 10,000 spectators. Cowboys' officials tried unsuccessfully to generate interest in the team. Midway through the first year, officials sent several players to the State Fair of Texas, in Dallas, to sign autographs and give away Cowboy keychains.

"We sat out there a couple of hours, trying to give away trinkets and pictures, and nobody wanted them," said running back Don McIlhenny.

The Cowboys were hurt by competition from the Dallas Texans, of the new American Football League. The Texans, like the Cowboys, began play in 1960, and both teams called the Cotton Bowl their home. But the Texans drew larger crowds and generated more interest, largely because they were exciting and won games. The Texans finished 8–6 their first year, with an outstanding roster that included future AFL stars Len Dawson, Jerry Mays, and E.J. Holub.

"I was a big Texans fan, and so were all my friends," said Cowboys' fullback Walt Garrison, who grew up in a Dallas suburb. "We didn't go to any Cowboy games."

Both the Cowboys and Texans lost money their first year. Clint Murchison Jr., the Cowboys' owner, and Lamar Hunt, the Texans' owner, each hoped the other would abandon the market. Murchison got his wish when Hunt moved the Texans to Kansas City before the 1963 season, and renamed them the Chiefs.

But even without the Texans as competition, the Cowboys drew few fans. The first sellout wouldn't occur for another five years. The future looked bleak.

3 Tex Schramm

More than anyone else, Tex Schramm built the Dallas Cowboys. Texas Earnest Schramm Jr. was born in California. He came to the Lone Star State in 1939 to attend the University of Texas. After graduating in 1947 he went to work for the Los Angeles Rams and rose to the position of general manager. Later he worked for CBS television in New York.

The Cowboys' owner, Clint Murchison Jr., hired Schramm as general manager in 1959, on the advice of Chicago Bears' owner George Halas. Murchison, who was a hands-off owner, turned over the club's operation to Schramm, who loved the challenge.

"As far back as I can remember, I dreamed of the opportunity to take a team from scratch and build it," Schramm said.

He made a series of brilliant moves early on. First, he hired Tom Landry as coach. At the time, Landry was defensive coordinator for the New York Giants, and had no head coaching experience. But he was a highly regarded assistant with a brilliant mind. Once he came to the Cowboys, Landry developed multiple-set offenses and complex defenses that revolutionized professional football.

Schramm also hired Gil Brandt as player personnel director. Brandt, who had been a part-time scout for the Rams, had a remarkable eye for talent. During his long career with the Cowboys, he consistently found unheralded players at small, out-of-the-way colleges who blossomed into stars. Schramm's influence even extended to naming the team.

"Before we got the franchise, we planned to name the team the Dallas Steers," he said. "But after thinking about it, nobody liked the idea of a castrated bull."

From the beginning, Schramm marketed the Cowboys brilliantly. He understood the potential of television while it was still in its infancy, and he got the Cowboys on the air as much as possible.

"We would always play whenever they wanted us for a national telecast," Schramm said. "As a result, we got more exposure down through the years than any other team."

Schramm had many talents, but he could also be difficult. People called him stubborn, arrogant, and impatient for good reason. He had a reputation for being cheap with salaries. Lee Roy Jordan, the team's star middle linebacker of the 1960s and '70s, often butted heads with Schramm over his pay. He once staged a brief holdout before finally receiving a new contract.

Schramm quickly rose to great power within the NFL. Along with commissioner Pete Rozelle, Schramm negotiated the merger between the American Football League and the National Football League that took effect in the 1970 season. Later, Schramm came up with innovations such as sudden-death overtime, the wild-card playoff format, and instant replay.

Schramm resigned from the Cowboys in 1989, two months after Jerry Jones bought the team from its second owner, Bum Bright. In 1991, Schramm was voted into the Pro Football Hall of Fame. In 2003, he received another honor when Jones inducted Schramm into the team's

Ring of Honor at Texas Stadium.

Schramm joined legendary players such as Bob Lilly, Roger Staubach, Tony Dorsett, and Randy White. Jones said he wanted to put aside any hard feelings from his takeover, and acknowledge Schramm's immense team contributions.

"Tex will always be recognized ... as the architect and the man who started and built the Cowboys into America's Team," Jones said.

4 Tom Landry—Early Years

NFL coaches usually don't last long. If a coach has a losing season or two, he often gets sent packing. Lasting 29 years, the second-longest tenure of any coach with an NFL team, Tom Landry proved to be the exception.

But in the early years, Landry's job security seemed shaky. In his first season in 1960, Landry didn't win a game. After four seasons, he had only a 13–38–3 record. Dallas fans were becoming impatient with losing.

"People were getting tired of waiting till next year," general manager Tex Schramm said. "They were ready for us to start winning, and there was a growing list of people around town who had decided we weren't going to be able to do so with the coach we had."

Owner Clint Murchison Jr. stood by Landry. He silenced speculation about Landry's future by rewarding him with an unprecedented 10-year contract extension in 1964. Landry was as surprised as anyone by the vote of confidence.

"I fully expected to be fired at some point, knowing that it would probably take longer to build the team than most felt it would take," Landry said.

Ironically, Landry wasn't even sure he wanted the job in the first place. He was defensive coordinator for the New York Giants, and was rumored to be their next head coach when Schramm offered him the Dallas job before the 1960 season.

Landry wasn't looking to move, but he liked the idea of returning to

Tom Landry is greeted at the airport in Dallas by Dallas Cowboys general manager Tex Schramm in late December 1959.

Flying High

Tom Landry faced plenty of pressure as Cowboys' coach. But as a 19-year-old fighter pilot in World War II, he faced death. Landry flew 30 combat missions with the Army Air Corps between his freshman and sophomore years at the University of Texas.

"War tested me, but I survived," Landry said. "And that experience gave me not only a broader perspective on life, but a confidence in myself I had never known before."

Texas. He had grown up in South Texas and attended the University of Texas on a football scholarship. After college, he played defensive back for the Giants from 1950 to 1955 before retiring and joining the coaching staff. Landry lived in Dallas during the off-season and sold insurance. He expected insurance, not football, to be his eventual career.

"I knew becoming head coach of a new team wouldn't be a very secure position," Landry said. "And yet, a head coaching job in Dallas, even if it lasted only two, maybe three years, could buy me the time I needed to build my business to the point I could adequately support my family."

Landry never built up his insurance business. Shortly after signing the long contract extension, he turned the Cowboys into a winner. In 1965, they finished 7–7, their first non-losing season. In 1966, they improved to 10–3–1, and advanced to the NFL Championship Game against the legendary Green Bay Packers. The Cowboys lost, 34–27, but played well and had a chance to win.

In 1967, the Cowboys earned a rematch with the Packers, and again, fought until the end. This time, they lost 21–17 in the closing seconds of the infamous Ice Bowl. Despite the narrow defeats, Dallas had made a meteoric rise from the bottom of the NFL to the top.

Landry accounted for much of the success. He was a different breed of head coach. He was quiet and studious, more like a college professor than a fire-and-brimstone coach. He rarely yelled at players or screamed at officials.

During games, he normally kept a stoic impression. He didn't overreact to good plays or bad plays. Like a chess player, he was always pondering his next move.

"If you're calling plays on the sidelines, you don't have time to be emotional," Landry said. "Anytime you show emotion, your concentration or train of thought is broken."

Even his clothing conveyed order and control. Landry always wore a well-tailored sport coat, tie, and his trademark fedora during games. He could have passed for the CEO of a Fortune 500 company. His appearance mirrored the preparation he put into each game.

"Coach Landry prepared us so well," said Dan Reeves, a running back and later assistant coach. "There are very few times I can remember us being surprised or not ready for something."

5 Ice Bowl

The Cowboys faced two formidable opponents in the 1967 NFL Championship Game: the Green Bay Packers and the weather. No game had ever been played in such inhospitable conditions. At kickoff, the temperature in Green Bay was 13 below zero. A blustery wind made it feel even colder. Players weren't prepared for the brutal cold, because the day before, temperatures had hovered around 20 degrees—balmy by comparison. Cowboys players scrambled to find ways to stay warm before the game.

"I put on two pairs of longjohns and wrapped Saran wrap around my feet," Cowboys' defensive lineman Bob Lilly said.

Packers' guard Jerry Kramer, who was used to playing in frigid weather, said he felt a little sorry for the Cowboys.

"As bad as the cold was for us, it had to be worse for them," Kramer said. "They were all hunched over, rubbing their hands, moving their legs up and down, trying to persuade themselves that they weren't insane to be playing football in this ridiculous weather."

The cold hurt the Cowboys' game plan because they relied on complex formations and a wide-open offense. The unsure footing of frozen Lambeau Field neutralized the Cowboys' biggest advantage, speed. The

Packers, by contrast, used a basic, straight-ahead running game that emphasized power over speed. Their game wasn't hurt as much by a field that resembled an ice-skating rink.

The Packers, as expected, dominated early. They took a 14–0 lead on two Bart Starr touchdown passes, but the Cowboys quickly battled back. Defensive end George Andrie hit Starr in the pocket and forced a fumble. Andrie recovered the ball and rumbled seven yards for a touchdown. The Cowboys also added a field goal before halftime.

In the third quarter, neither team could score. Meanwhile, temperatures got even colder, plummeting to 20 below. Few Green Bay fans left the stadium. They huddled in blankets, parkas, and ski masks, trying to leave no skin exposed to the arctic conditions. Early in the fourth quarter, the Cowboys surprised the Packers with a 50-yard touchdown pass from halfback Dan Reeves to receiver Lance Rentzel. The extra point put Dallas ahead, 17–14. Packer fans, not to mention Cowboy fans, were stunned. Dallas had reeled off 17 straight points, but the veteran Packers weren't through.

With 4:50 left in the game, the Packers began a drive at their own 32-yard line. Starr went to work, completing short passes to his running backs, who managed to keep their footing and pick up first down after first down. After nine plays, the Packers had moved all the way to the Dallas 1-yard line. They had a first down, and victory seemed imminent. The Cowboys, however, mounted a stellar defense, stopping the Packers twice.

Now the Packers faced third down with only 16 seconds remaining. Starr called the team's last timeout to confer with coach Vince Lombardi. Dallas defenders tried to dig their cleats into the ice and stop them one more time. If Green Bay tried a run and didn't score, the clock would run out.

Starr brought the Packers to the line. He took the snap, tucked the ball against his chest, lowered his head and plowed forward. His linemen opened a small crease in the Dallas defense, and Starr squeezed into the end zone to win the game. Final score: Packers 21, Cowboys 17.

For the second straight year, Dallas had suffered a devastating defeat to the Packers in the title game. But this loss was even harder to handle.

"We were so close," Rentzel said.

6 Blooper Bowl

The back-to-back championship losses to Green Bay in 1966 and 1967 had branded the Cowboys as a team that couldn't win the big game. That reputation was reinforced when Dallas suffered early-round playoff losses in 1968 and 1969.

In 1970, however, the Cowboys looked like they might finally shake the monkey off their backs. Dallas compiled a 10–4 record, won two playoff games, and met the Baltimore Colts in Super Bowl V. The Cowboys seemed to match up well against the Colts, led by veteran quarterback Johnny Unitas. The Cowboys were deeper, younger, and faster.

The game began well for Dallas. Two field goals gave the Cowboys an early 6–0 lead, and their defense shut down the Colts. But Baltimore drew even on a freak play early in the second quarter. Unitas dropped back to pass and threw across the middle to receiver Eddie Hinton. The ball was high and deflected off his hands toward Dallas cornerback Mel Renfro. He appeared to tip it, then the ball landed in the arms of Colts' tight end John Mackey who rumbled 75 yards for a touchdown. Dallas vigorously protested the touchdown.

Renfro insisted he didn't touch the ball. If he hadn't, the play would be called back. The rules said one offensive player couldn't tip the ball to a teammate without a defender first touching it. But the officials stood by their call and awarded Baltimore a touchdown. Dallas blocked the extra point to keep the game tied, 6–6.

The Cowboys quickly bounced back. Defensive end George Andrie hit Unitas, knocked the ball loose, and recovered it on the Colts' 29-yard line. Quarterback Craig Morton directed a drive that ended with a 7-yard touchdown pass to running back Duane Thomas. Dallas had seized a 13–6 halftime lead.

The Cowboys received more good fortune on the second half opening kickoff. The Colts' Jim Duncan fumbled the kick, and Dallas recovered on the Baltimore 31-yard line. Five plays later, Dallas had moved to the 2. Thomas then took a handoff, but had the ball stripped inches from the goal line.

Cowboys' center Dave Manders seemed to recover the ball. But amid the pile of bodies, officials awarded possession to the Colts. For the second time in the game, the Cowboys felt robbed by the referees. Manders was livid. He emerged from the pile, holding the ball high to prove he had it. But Baltimore lineman Billy Ray Smith did a marvelous sales job, yelling "Our ball! Our ball!" amid the confusion.

The Cowboys tried to regroup, knowing they had missed a chance to put the game away with a touchdown. In the third quarter, neither team scored. Midway through the fourth quarter, Dallas still clung to a precarious 13–6 lead. The Cowboys took possession on their own 27-yard line, hoping to mount a long, time-consuming drive. But Morton tossed a short pass to fullback Walt Garrison that deflected off his fingertips. Colts' safety Rick Volk intercepted and returned the ball to the Dallas 3-yard line.

Again, Dallas faced adversity. Baltimore quickly scored to tie the game, 13–13. With only two minutes remaining, Dallas had a first down at the Baltimore 48-yard line. They seemed in prime position to win. The Cowboys needed only a couple of first downs to be in position to kick a game-winning field goal.

But Morton again committed a blunder. He tossed a wobbly pass to half-back Dan Reeves that skimmed off his fingers and into the arms of Colts' linebacker Mike Curtis. He ran the ball back to the Dallas 28-yard line with just over a minute remaining. The Colts had a chance to win. They called two running plays to get the ball in field goal range.

With only five seconds left, rookie kicker Jim O'Brien lined up for a 32-yard attempt. He had missed an earlier field goal attempt, but this was one was successful. The Colts won, 16–13.

Despite dominating the game, the Cowboys had suffered another devastating big-game loss. In frustration, defensive lineman Bob Lilly hurled his helmet 40 yards down the field after the final whistle.

"To lose that game like we did was the lowest point of my career," he said.

Unlikely MVP

The Cowboys had nothing to celebrate after their bumbling 16–13 loss to the Baltimore Colts in Super Bowl V. But one player, linebacker Chuck Howley, received an award normally reserved for a member of the winning team.

Howley was named the game's Most Valuable Player for intercepting two passes and recovering a fumble. The award included a new 1971 Dodge Charger, a popular muscle car of the day. Howley's delighted wife was photographed next to the car.

Howley would have much preferred a Super Bowl win.

The game was dubbed the "Blooper Bowl" because of the sloppy play by both teams. They combined for 11 turnovers—seven by the Colts and four by the Cowboys. The mistakes deepened the painful loss. The Cowboys had missed a golden opportunity to shed the unwanted nickname of Next Year's Champion.

7 Redemption

The Cowboys had one more chance at redemption in Super Bowl VI. The 16–13 loss in Super Bowl V continued a record of failure in championship games.

This time, the Cowboys had a new quarterback, Roger Staubach. He had taken over as starter midway through the 1971 season. Staubach engineered seven straight wins and two playoff victories.

The Cowboys had become a dominant team, and were favored over the Miami Dolphins. But the Cowboys had found creative ways to lose title games before. Would this year be any different? They didn't take the Dolphins lightly. Miami had an arsenal of offensive weapons, starting with quarterback Bob Griese. He could throw to speedy receiver Paul Warfield or hand off to a trio of talented backs: Larry Csonka, Jim Kiick, and Mercury Morris.

The first quarter started off well for the Cowboys. They recovered a Csonka fumble and quickly kicked a field goal to lead 3–0. In the second quarter, they extended their lead to 10–0 when Staubach hit receiver Lance Alworth for a 7-yard touchdown. The Dolphins responded with a field goal just before halftime to cut the Dallas lead to 10–3.

In the second half, the Cowboys began to control the game. They took the opening kickoff and drove 71 yards for a touchdown, capped by a 3-yard run by Duane Thomas. The Dolphins couldn't stop the Cowboys' powerful running game. Thomas and fellow backs Calvin Hill and Walt Garrison combined for 194 of the Cowboys' 252 yards rushing.

In the fourth quarter, Staubach threw a 7-yard touchdown pass to tight end Mike Ditka to widen the lead to 24–3. Neither team scored again, and Dallas finally had its first world championship. The Dolphins became the first Super Bowl team to fail to score a touchdown.

Defensive tackle Bob Lilly, who threw his helmet in frustration at the end of Super Bowl V, made the signature play of Super Bowl VI. He relentlessly chased Griese, sacking him for a 29-yard loss in the first quarter. "It was a big play because it made a statement," Lilly said. "They were going to lose."

Throughout the 1971 season, players were on a mission to finally win the Super Bowl. Despite the naysayers, they believed in themselves. When the Cowboys finally achieved their goal, many said they felt more relief than joy.

"All that frustration of being runner-up finally was lifted off our backs," Lilly said.

Landry said he felt confident the Cowboys would finally win the big one. "You could see it in the players' eyes," he said. "We were determined nobody was going to stop us."

Staubach won the Most Valuable Player award, thanks to completing 12 of 19 passes and throwing two touchdowns. With the win, he silenced any quarterback controversy in Dallas. The Cowboys were now his team. He would lead them to three other Super Bowl appearances in the 1970s, and become the greatest quarterback in team history.

8 Tom Landry—Later Years

The Landry Era began with a string of losing seasons, and it ended with a string of losing seasons. In between, Landry led the Cowboys to five Super Bowl appearances and 20 consecutive winning seasons.

But for all of his success, Landry couldn't prevent the team's steep decline in the mid-1980s. The nosedive began with a 7–9 record in 1986. It continued with a 7–8 mark in 1987, and worsened with an abysmal 3–13 record in 1988. Owner Bum Bright, who bought the team in 1984, was growing impatient with Landry.

He began to publicly criticize him, saying Landry's play calling was "horrendous." Bright urged general manager Tex Schramm, who had hired Landry back in 1960, to fire him but Schramm resisted.

"I knew it should be done," he said. "The only reason I didn't is that we started together, and I felt a loyalty to him."

How did the Cowboys, a model of consistency, fall to the league's bottom? The decline began gradually, almost imperceptibly. First of all, age caught up with the Cowboys. By the mid-1980s, quarterback Danny White, running back Tony Dorsett, and defensive tackle Randy White were all in their thirties and nearing retirement.

Second, the Cowboys made a series of draft mistakes, picking players who turned out to be busts. They couldn't plug in young, developing players for stars past their prime. The Cowboys had a 20-year history of drafting success, so most of their top picks had long, productive careers.

By the early 1980s, the drafting mojo was gone. For example, the Cowboys drafted Rod Hill with their top pick in 1982. Hill, a defensive back from little Kentucky State, lasted only two seasons and never made an impact. He epitomized the decade's drafting disasters.

Other failed No. 1 draft picks included linebacker Billy Cannon Jr. (1984), defensive tackle Kevin Brooks (1985), receiver Mike Sherrard

Landry's Record

Tom Landry's firing didn't diminish his legacy as one of the greatest coaches in NFL history. He finished with 270 wins, behind only George Halas of the Chicago Bears and Don Shula of the Baltimore Colts and Miami Dolphins.

Landry's 29 years with the Cowboys ranks as the second-longest coaching tenure with one team. In 1990, a year after leaving the Cowboys, Landry was inducted into the Pro Football Hall of Fame.

In 1994, he accepted Jerry Jones' offer to be included in the Cowboys Ring of Honor at Texas Stadium. Jones had made the offer several years earlier, but Landry declined. Some former players finally persuaded Landry to accept the honor.

His name is now listed alongside great players such as Don Meredith, Roger Staubach, Bob Lilly, and Tony Dorsett. No one deserves to be in the Ring of Honor more than Landry.

(1986), and defensive tackle Danny Noonan (1987).

Many believed as the talent deteriorated, so did Landry's coaching ability. He stubbornly held onto offensive and defensive systems, such as the flex defense, that no longer were effective. Schramm privately hoped Landry would retire. When he didn't, Schramm began to make moves to hasten his exit. He hired Paul Hackett, a highly regarded offensive coordinator for the San Francisco 49ers, to lead the Dallas offense. Schramm envisioned Hackett as an eventual successor to Landry.

But a power struggle ensued. Landry didn't want to hand over the offense to Hackett. He eventually persuaded Schramm to give him a new three-year contract in 1987.

"I signed that contract because I thought it would take three years to get this thing turned around," Landry said.

He never got to finish the job. In 1989, Arkansas oilman Jerry Jones bought the Cowboys and abruptly fired Landry. He did what Schramm couldn't. Landry said a tearful goodbye to his players.

"I'd experienced a lot of low times in my career," Landry wrote in his 1990 autobiography. "This was the biggest. Worse than any playoff loss marking the sudden end of a season. After this, there were no more seasons."

9 Jerry Jones Takes Over

When he arrived in 1989, Jerry Jones shook up the team and the town. Fans were accustomed to low-key owners, such as Clint Murchison Jr. and Bum Bright, who were content to bankroll a winner and let the players make the headlines.

Not Jones. As soon as he bought the team, he became the unmistakable face of the Cowboys. His first and biggest move was firing legendary coach Tom Landry. After purchasing the team from Bright, Jones hopped on a private plane and flew to Austin, where Landry was vacationing with his family. Jones brought along Tex Schramm, the Cowboys' longtime general manager, to witness the sudden firing.

Landry said Jones told him bluntly that he had bought the team and wanted Jimmy Johnson to be his coach.

"I don't remember much of anything he said after that," Landry wrote in his autobiography. "A jumble of feelings crowded my mind: anger, sadness, frustration, disappointment, resignation."

Schramm shared many of those feelings.

"It was a very difficult meeting," he said. "It's tough when you break a relationship you've had for 29 years."

After the hastily scheduled meeting, Jones flew back to Dallas for a press conference to announce his purchase. Jones had little experience with the media, and it showed. He came across as brash, instead of respectful of the Cowboys' rich past.

"We must win," Jones said excitedly. "We will win. Winning is the name of the game."

He declared that he would be a hands-on owner, involved in everything from "socks to jocks." He told reporters that Johnson, who had won a national championship at the University of Miami, would be worth "five No. 1 draft choices."

Tom Landry Day

After Landry was fired, Cowboy fans responded with an outpouring of support. More than 50,000 people lined the streets of downtown Dallas for a "Hats Off to Tom Landry Parade." People held up dozens of signs reading "Tom Landry—Thanks for 29 Great Years" and "Landry for Governor."

Landry and his wife, Alicia, rode in a convertible and waved to the crowd.

"We love you, Coach," people cried.

Cowboy greats such as Roger Staubach, Tony Dorsett, and Drew Pearson rode in the parade. The Texas governor and Dallas mayor attended, and President George Bush and evangelist Billy Graham sent telegrams of support.

"I don't deserve this," Landry said. "But I am so thankful for it."

Many fans were stunned and angered by Jones' lightning-quick changes. They may have grown disillusioned with Landry, but they didn't think he deserved to be tossed aside so coldly. Landry became a martyr and Jones the bad guy.

Jones would later admit he botched the firing of Landry. But at the time he didn't seem concerned about people's feelings.

"You could tell right from the beginning that he didn't give a damn about history," Schramm said. "You can tell this man has absolutely no feeling for the past. You almost expected him to take the stars off the helmets."

10 1–15

Jimmy Johnson didn't like the roster he inherited as the Cowboys' head coach. He said the University of Miami team he left could have beaten the 1989 Cowboys.

"I'd always held the Cowboys in such high regard, almost on a pedestal," Johnson said. " I was a little dismayed at what I saw on the field."

Johnson, like new owner Jerry Jones, was urgent to dismantle and rebuild the team. He cut veteran players and encouraged others, such as quarterback Danny White and defensive tackle Randy White, to retire. Johnson didn't promise the Cowboys would win immediately, and they didn't. However, he was confident he had set them on the right course.

In his first game, the Cowboys were shut out by the New Orleans Saints, 28–0. Other losses quickly followed, with games not even close. In one three-week stretch, the Cowboys lost 30–7, 30–13 and 31–13. They finished the year 1–15.

Johnson started rookie quarterback Troy Aikman, the team's prized No. 1 draft pick. Behind a weak offensive line, Aikman took a beating week after week. He looked lost at times, and threw more interceptions than touchdowns, but he also showed signs of future greatness.

For instance, Aikman threw for 379 yards, a rookie record, in a 24–20 loss to the Phoenix Cardinals. Three weeks later, Aikman threw four touchdown passes in a 35–31 loss to the St. Louis Rams. Aikman, despite the mounting losses, consistently showed toughness and leadership. He never made excuses for losing.

"A quarterback has to win," Aikman said.

One of the Cowboys' few strengths in 1989 was the running game. Herschel Walker, a former Heisman Trophy winner, possessed an unmatched combination of power and speed. He signed with the Cowboys in 1986 after the United States Football League folded.

In his first two seasons he split time with Tony Dorsett before Dorsett was traded to Denver. In 1988, as the showcase back, Walker had an All-Pro season rushing for 1,514 yards. He continued his torrid pace as the 1989 season began.

The Cowboys kept losing. Johnson knew that Walker alone couldn't turn Dallas into a winner, so Johnson made one of the biggest trades in NFL history. He sent Walker to the Minnesota Vikings for five players and eight draft picks.

The Cowboys had pulled off a heist. They used the draft picks to build a team that won three Super Bowl teams in the 1990s.

Minnesota had expected Walker to be the missing link to a Super Bowl title. Instead, he didn't come close to meeting expectations. He failed to gain 1,000 yards in 1989, 1990, or 1991. After the 1991 season, the Vikings released Walker, just as the Cowboys were on the brink of their first Super Bowl title since 1977.

The 1989 season was remembered as the year the Cowboys hit rock bottom, but it was also the year they planted the seeds of success.

11 Troy Aikman—Early Years

The Green Bay Packers did the Cowboys a huge favor on Dec. 18, 1988, the last day of the regular season. The lowly Packers beat the Phoenix Cardinals, 26–17.

Why did this game, while meaningless in the final standings, matter to the Cowboys? Because by winning, the Packers assured the Cowboys of having the league's worst record, and the right to the No. 1 pick in the upcoming draft.

The Cowboys used that pick to take Troy Aikman—the very man who would lead the Cowboys to three Super Bowl wins in the 1990s, and end up in the Hall of Fame.

If the Packers had, instead, lost their final game, Aikman probably would have spent his career in frigid Green Bay. It's hard to imagine Aikman wearing the green and gold of the Packers instead of the blue and silver of the Cowboys.

The Cowboys and every other NFL team coveted Aikman when he entered the draft. In two seasons at UCLA, Aikman had completed almost 65 percent of his passes, throwing 41 touchdowns and leading the Bruins to a 20–4 record. He had all the tools: size (6'3" and 218 pounds), a rifle arm, toughness, and intelligence.

Jimmy Johnson, in his first year as the Cowboys' coach, couldn't have asked for a better quarterback. Aikman would become the Cowboys' first

Troy Aikman poses with NFL commissioner Pete Rozelle at the 54th annual draft of collegiate talent. The UCLA quarterback was the first pick by the Dallas Cowboys and had already signed a six-year, $11.2 million contract with the Cowboys.

franchise quarterback since Roger Staubach, who retired a decade earlier. Aikman started as a rookie and had some great games and some awful ones. He threw twice as many interceptions as touchdowns, and the Cowboys limped to a 1–15 finish.

However, neither Johnson nor new owner Jerry Jones had any doubts about Aikman's potential—nor did others around the league. Aikman had all the skills for stardom. He only needed more experience. Fans, too, sensed that Aikman would be special.

"Troy came to this city at a time it was hungry for a winner," Johnson said. "He fit the mold beautifully."

Once a Sooner

Troy Aikman had such a stellar career at UCLA that it's easy to forget he started out playing for the University of Oklahoma. As a freshman in 1984, he broke into OU's starting lineup. In his second season, he and the Sooners were off to an undefeated start when Aikman broke his ankle in the fourth game.

Jamelle Holieway, a marvelous option quarterback, stepped in and led OU to the 1985 national championship. Oklahoma coach Barry Switzer, who had run the Wishbone offense for years, changed to a passing attack to accommodate Aikman's skills. But when Holieway produced a national championship, Switzer decided to revert to the option offense.

Aikman, who grew up in Henryetta, Oklahoma, was the odd man out. With Switzer's blessing, he transferred to UCLA the next year.

"I realized if I stayed with the Sooners, there was a good chance I'd be riding the bench my last two years in college," Aikman said.

Aikman improved each year, and so did the Cowboys. In 1991, his third season, he completed 65 percent of his passes, and the Cowboys finished 11–5, their best record since 1983. The Cowboys also made the playoffs for the first time since 1985, but lost in the second round.

Aikman and the Cowboys did even better in 1992. He threw a career-high 23 touchdowns, and the Cowboys rolled to a 13–3 record—the most wins in franchise history. They beat Philadelphia and San Francisco to advance to Super Bowl XXVII. It was the Cowboys' first Super Bowl appearance in 15 years, and they demolished the Buffalo Bills, 52–17. Aikman threw four touchdown passes and no interceptions. Not surprisingly, he was voted the game's Most Valuable Player.

Aikman's rapid ascent had been amazing. In only four seasons, he led the Cowboys from the NFL wilderness to the mountaintop and he kept them there. The next season, the Cowboys met the Bills again, in Super Bowl XXVIII. This time, Dallas thrashed Buffalo 30–13.

In 1994, the Cowboys lost to San Francisco in the NFC Championship Game, falling just short of a third straight Super Bowl appearance. But in 1995, Aikman and the Cowboys won another title, whipping the

Pittsburgh Steelers, 27–17, in Super Bowl XXX.

At this point, Aikman was only 29 years old. He already had Hall of Fame credentials, and his career was far from over.

12 Emmitt Smith

Today, it's hard to believe. But some scouts didn't think Emmitt Smith would be a star in the NFL. After all, he was short and not particularly fast. As a result, 16 teams passed over Smith in the 1990 draft. Jimmy Johnson, the Cowboys' second-year coach, immediately snapped up Smith with his first pick.

Johnson, as coach at the University of Miami, had followed Smith's remarkable career at Florida. Smith started as a freshman and set virtually all the school's rushing records, even though he left for the NFL after his junior season. Johnson was so certain of Smith's ability that he traded up in the draft to nab him. Smith became the Cowboys' most heralded rookie running back since Tony Dorsett in 1977.

"Emmitt Smith brings star quality to us," Johnson beamed.

Smith, however, missed his first training camp in a lengthy contract dispute. Some people wondered about his attitude. Days before the start of the 1990 season, Smith agreed to a three-year, $3 million contract. He played sparingly in the opening game, then started the next four games, producing only mediocre stats. In his first game as a starter, Smith gained only 11 yards. He followed up the next three games with 63, 28, and 30 yards.

Had the Cowboys made a huge mistake in drafting Smith? No. The next week, he eased concerns by rushing for 121 yards. Smith finished his rookie year with 937 yards, short of his goal of 1,000 yards.

"I had a decent first year, but it didn't satisfy me," Smith said.

In 1991, his second year, Smith led the league with 1,563 yards rushing, becoming the first Cowboy to ever win the rushing title. In 1992, Smith set a

Already showing signs of greatness, rookie Emmitt Smith leaps over a couple of Tampa Bay Buccaneers defenders on October 7, 1990.

franchise record with 1,713 yards, again leading the league. He played a critical role in the Cowboys' 13–3 record, and their 52–17 thumping of the Buffalo Bills in Super Bowl XXVII. Smith rushed for 108 yards in the blowout.

During his 13-year Dallas career, Smith won four NFL rushing titles and made the Pro Bowl eight times. He gained 17,162 yards, and easily surpassed the team record of 12,036 set by Tony Dorsett from 1977 to 1987. Smith and Dorsett, easily the best running backs in Dallas history, had dramatically different running styles. Dorsett, who weighed only 190 pounds, relied on breakaway speed and fluid moves to elude tacklers. Smith, a powerful 210 pounds, bounced off tacklers and churned for extra yardage.

In his final year as a Cowboy, Smith broke Walter Payton's all-time NFL rushing record of 16,726 yards. Smith set the new mark on October 27, 2002, against the Seattle Seahawks. He did so on an 11-yard run midway through the fourth quarter. The Cowboys lost, 17–14, when Seattle kicked a last-second field goal. But no one really cared. Fans had come to see Smith break the record.

After the season, the Cowboys chose not to re-sign Smith. They were looking to shed his big salary and to develop younger players. Smith played his final two seasons with the Arizona Cardinals, retiring in 2004. He didn't go out with a whimper either. In his last year, at age 35, Smith gained 937 yards. Ironically, that's the exact rushing total he had as a rookie.

Smith, no doubt, will be inducted into the Hall of Fame in his first year of eligibility in 2009. NFL teams that passed on Smith will kick themselves one more time.

13 Michael Irvin

They called him The Playmaker, and the nickname fit. Irvin defined his 12-year career with clutch catches for first downs and touchdowns. When he retired in 2000, he owned most of the team receiving records.

The Cowboys took Irvin with their first choice in the 1988 draft. He had starred at the University of Miami under coach Jimmy Johnson, who would later become the Cowboys' coach. In his first year, Irvin broke into the starting lineup—the first rookie receiver to do so since the legendary Bob Hayes.

In his second year, Irvin hooked up with rookie quarterback Troy Aikman, and their careers took off together. Irvin starred in all three of the Cowboys' 1990s Super Bowl wins. He had his best game in the first one, Super Bowl XXVII. He caught six passes for 114 yards, and scored two

Michael Irvin celebrates a touchdown during the NFC Championship Game against the Green Bay Packers on January 14, 1996.

touchdowns in a 52–17 blowout of the Buffalo Bills.

Irvin didn't have blazing speed, but his size (6'2" and 205 pounds) made him hard to bring down. He ran precise patterns and gained much of his yardage after the catch. Regardless of the game's importance, Irvin played with enthusiasm and determination. He became a leader on the field and in the locker room.

In 2007, Irvin received football's highest honor: induction into the Pro

Home Team

Irvin was one of 17 children raised by Walter and Pearl Irvin in a three-bedroom home in Fort Lauderdale, Fla. His father, a roofer and lay preacher, died when Michael was 17 years old. He took the loss hard. His father was strict but loving, making sure the kids went to bed on time and stayed in school.

"He was Superman," Michael said. "He'd get up at 6 or 7 o'clock in the morning and come home at 8 o'clock at night, six days a week, then he'd go preach on Sundays."

Money was tight at the Irvin household. Sometimes, the kids had to cut the toes out of their tennis shoes when they became too small, instead of buying new ones. The Irvins may have been poor financially, but they weren't poor in spirit. Michael's mother said she never regretted having such a large family.

"I don't know if life would have been simpler if we hadn't so many," she said. "I don't think life is ever meant to be simple."

Football Hall of Fame. He became only the eighth Cowboy player so honored, and the team's first receiver.

His stats merited selection. During his career, Irvin had 750 catches for 11,904 yards and was named to five straight Pro Bowls. Irvin, Aikman, and running back Emmitt Smith became known as the Triplets. No team had a better offensive trio. Many people call the Cowboys of the early 1990s the greatest team in NFL history, and Irvin played a huge role.

"He was the guy who I knew I could depend on to come through with a key play," Coach Johnson said. "He never shied away from making the tough catch."

Irvin's career came to an abrupt, premature end on October 10, 1999. In a road game against the Philadelphia Eagles, Irvin caught a slant pass across the middle. His head slammed against the artificial turf, and he lay motionless for several minutes before being carried off on a stretcher. He suffered a spinal injury and never played again.

No one could question Irvin's on-the-field performance, but his off-the-field behavior occasionally got him in trouble. In 1996, he pleaded guilty to felony drug possession and received five years' probation and 100 hours of community service. The NFL suspended him for the first five games of the 1996 season. In an emotional Hall of Fame acceptance speech, Irvin apologized for his conduct.

Coaches and teammates, however, remember his highlights. Almost a decade has passed since Irvin retired, and no Cowboy receiver has matched his impact.

"I never coached a player who has as much passion for the game as Michael Irvin," Johnson said.

14 Super Bowl XXVII—A Rout

Cowboys coach Jimmy Johnson never doubted the Cowboys would win Super Bowl XXVII. His confidence carried over to the players.

"We said all year that our best game was going to be the last game of the year," Johnson said.

He looked like a prophet. The Cowboys humiliated the Buffalo Bills in the Super Bowl, 52–17. But early on Johnson's confidence looked misplaced. The Bills took a 7–0 lead on a 2-yard run by Thurman Thomas. The Cowboys, however, were undeterred. Quarterback Troy Aikman led a drive that ended with a 23-yard touchdown pass to tight end Jay Novacek near the end of the first quarter.

The Cowboys wasted no time in scoring again. On Buffalo's next possession, Dallas defensive end Charles Haley sacked quarterback Jim Kelly near the Bills' end zone. Kelly fumbled, and defensive lineman Jimmie Jones scooped up the ball and ran 2 yards for a touchdown. Dallas now had a 14–7 lead.

Buffalo, however, didn't roll over. Early in the second quarter, the Bills cut the lead to 14–10 with a 21-yard field goal. But they would never draw closer. The Cowboys broke open the game with an offensive onslaught. Aikman hit receiver Michael Irvin on two touchdown passes only 18 seconds apart in the second quarter. The touchdowns gave Dallas a 28–10 halftime lead and unstoppable momentum.

Leon's Lapse

The Cowboys' 52–17 annihilation of the Bills should have been even worse.

Dallas defensive lineman Leon Lett came within inches of scoring a touchdown that would have given the Cowboys the largest margin of victory ever in a Super Bowl.

Lett recovered a fumble at the Cowboys' 35-yard line late in the game, and began rumbling down the field for what looked like a certain touchdown. Lett, 6' 6" and 287 pounds, became so overcome with joy that he began to showboat, holding the football low to the ground as he neared the goal line.

Buffalo receiver Don Beebe, unwilling to see Dallas add to its widening lead, raced up behind Lett and slapped the ball out of his hands. It bounced through the end zone, and the Bills took over at their 20-yard line.

Lett walked sheepishly to the sidelines.

"No need in chewing out Leon," Coach Johnson said. "He felt bad enough. Suffice it to say he would never celebrate prematurely again."

Midway through the third quarter, the Cowboys extended their lead to 31–10 on a 20-yard field goal. Buffalo then scored its final touchdown of the game, a 40-yard touchdown pass from backup quarterback Frank Reich. He was subbing for Kelly, who had gone out with an injury.

In the fourth quarter, the Cowboys weren't content to sit on their 31–17 lead. They peppered the Bills with three more touchdowns. Receiver Alvin Harper caught a 45-yard touchdown pass. Emmitt Smith scored on a 10-yard run, and linebacker Ken Norton Jr. picked up a fumble and ran nine yards for a touchdown.

Final score: Dallas 52, Buffalo 17. No Super Bowl winner had ever looked more dominant.

"Dallas Cowboys, world champions," owner Jerry Jones kept repeating after the game.

The Super Bowl win capped a remarkable four-year turnaround for the Cowboys. In 1989, Johnson's first year, the Cowboys had the league's worst record, 1–15. They improved every year, finishing 13–3 in 1992 on the way to the Cowboys' first Super Bowl triumph in 15 years.

The Cowboys won two more Super Bowls over the next three seasons, but the first was the sweetest.

15 Bob Lilly

Bob Lilly holds a special place in Dallas Cowboys history. The defensive tackle was the team's first-ever draft choice in 1961. He was selected to more Pro Bowl teams (11) than any other Cowboy. He also was the first Cowboy to be inducted into the Pro Football Hall of Fame.

Lilly earned his nickname, Mr. Cowboy. During the 1960s and early '70s, he terrorized opposing offenses, becoming the most dominant lineman of his era. Lilly, 6' 5" and 260 pounds, had extraordinary strength and quickness. Opposing teams routinely double-teamed Lilly, but he still stopped runners for no gain and sacked quarterbacks for big losses.

Lilly even managed to score four touchdowns. One came on an interception and three on fumble returns.

"He is the greatest player I ever coached," Tom Landry said. "He's that once-in-a-lifetime player."

Lilly missed only one game in his 14-year career. He went about his job, never taunting opponents or celebrating wildly after a big play.

"Bob didn't try to injure anyone," middle linebacker Lee Roy Jordan said. "Bob would tackle quarterbacks and lay them on the ground. Other guys would tackle them and throw them onto the AstroTurf with their 300-pound bodies and maybe break a rib or shoulder or something."

Off the field, Lilly was a gentle giant with a ready smile. His hobby was photography, and he became accomplished enough to sell his work in galleries.

Lilly grew up on a farm in Throckmorton, Texas, about three hours west of Dallas. He developed his legendary strength by tossing hay bales as a teenager. He attended Texas Christian University on a football scholarship and earned All-American honors as a junior and senior. Once, as a stunt, he lifted a Volkswagen onto a sidewalk, one end at a time.

Lilly joined the Cowboys in their second year, and he suffered through the bleak years before they became a perennial winner. He anchored the feared Doomsday Defense of the late 1960s and played in the back-to-back title game losses to the Green Bay Packers in 1966 and 1967. In the latter, the legendary Ice Bowl, Green Bay quarterback Bart Starr scored on a one-yard run in the dying seconds to give the Packers a 21–17 victory.

Lilly and the Cowboys suffered one of their most devastating defeats in Super Bowl V. They fell to the Baltimore Colts, 16–13, on a 32-yard field goal as time expired. Lilly, in frustration, threw his helmet 40 yards down the field as the game ended. Lilly and the Cowboys finally vindicated themselves in Super Bowl VI. They crushed the Miami Dolphins, 24–3, and Lilly had one of the most spectacular plays: a 29-yard quarterback sack.

Lilly played three more years, retiring in 1974. The next year, fittingly, he became the first player enshrined in the Cowboys Ring of Honor at Texas Stadium. In 1980, Lilly was inducted into the Pro Football Hall of Fame and later named to the NFL's 75th Anniversary Team.

Lilly contributed to the Cowboys' early success more than any other player. Mr. Cowboy will always be remembered.

16 Randy White

Randy White had a great nickname: the Manster. It stood for half-man, half-monster. Teammate Charlie Waters gave White the name early in his career, and it stuck. White played with an unmatched intensity.

The Cowboys made him their No. 1 draft choice in 1975 out of Maryland. At 6' 4" and 257 pounds, White was small for an NFL defensive lineman. For two years, the Cowboys tried to convert him into a middle linebacker. With White's speed and strength, coaches envisioned him revolutionizing the position.

White never made the adjustment. He liked being on the defensive line where he could react instinctively to the ball, instead of having to remember his assignment as linebacker. Finally, coaches gave up their

Randy White and defensive end Harvey Martin shared the Most Valuable Player award at Super Bowl XII in New Orleans on January 15, 1978.

experiment and returned White to tackle.

"I never did feel comfortable playing linebacker," White said. "Those first two years I was fighting for my life out there."

White flourished on the line. In 1977, he made 118 tackles, and the Cowboys flattened the Denver Broncos, 27–10, in Super Bowl XII. White and defensive end Harvey Martin were named co-Most Valuable Players. The Dallas defense dominated the Broncos, forcing four fumbles and holding them to 156 yards in total offense.

In 1978, White was named the NFC Defensive Player of the Year. He remained one of the league's dominant defensive tackles into the early 1980s. White had two distinct personalities. Off the field, he was kind and gentle. On the field, he transformed into a ruthless hitting machine.

"He's just mean," Martin once said. "That's all you can say."

White missed only one game in his 14-year career. He made the Pro Bowl nine times. Few linemen have ever been faster. White once made an astonishing play, tackling a receiver 49 yards downfield.

White was often compared to Bob Lilly, the team's dominant defensive tackle of an earlier era. Lilly was bigger, but White played with even more ferocity.

"He was one of those guys whom you were just thankful was on your side when the fight started," Waters said. "He scared me while I was in the huddle, so I just never talked to him. He had a wild, hateful look in his eye."

White retired before the 1989 season, shortly after Jimmy Johnson replaced Tom Landry as the Cowboys' coach. White wanted to keep playing, but Johnson urged him to retire to make room for younger players. White's reckless style of play had taken its toll on his body, although he wouldn't admit it.

"In the spring of 1989, watching Randy White trying to get into a stance was about like watching me trying to get into a stance," Johnson said.

White was inducted into the Pro Football Hall of Fame in 1994. Since then, he's had plenty of time for hunting and fishing, his two favorite pastimes. He still misses football.

"I've never found anything that has given me the thrill that I had right before a football game," White said.

17 Danny White

Danny White never got the respect he deserved. He had the misfortune of following Roger Staubach, the team's greatest quarterback ever.

White backed up Staubach for four years, then stepped into the starting role when Staubach retired after the 1979 season. White did exceptionally well. In his first year, he completed almost 60 percent of his passes and threw 28 touchdowns, breaking Staubach's touchdown record. White led the Cowboys to a 12–4 record and a wild-card spot in the playoffs. Under White, the Cowboys set a team record for points scored in 1980.

In 1981, he followed up with another solid season. He threw 22 touchdowns and led the Cowboys to another 12–4 finish. They beat their two biggest divisional rivals, Philadelphia and Washington, twice each. The 1982 season was shortened to nine games because of a players' strike. The Cowboys finished 6–3, and White again played well, completing 63 percent of his passes and throwing 16 touchdowns.

White, however, never took the Cowboys to a Super Bowl. Staubach, by comparison, led the team to four Super Bowls. As a result, White always remained in Staubach's shadow.

Some of White's outstanding performances tend to be forgotten. In 1980, he led the Cowboys to a thrilling come-from-behind win over the Atlanta Falcons in the divisional championship. The Cowboys had trailed 27–17 with less than four minutes remaining. White then led a frantic comeback, throwing two touchdown passes to receiver Drew Pearson. The last came with only 49 seconds left, to give Dallas a 30–27 win. The Cowboys, however, lost the next week to Philadelphia in the NFC Championship, one game shy of the Super Bowl.

In 1981 and 1982, the Cowboys again lost in the NFC Championship Game. White kept bringing the team tantalizingly close to the Super Bowl, but they kept falling just short. The next year, the Cowboys lost in the first round of the playoffs. Fans began to clamor for a change at quarterback.

Coach Tom Landry had always been a staunch White supporter. But swayed by public opinion, he named backup Gary Hogeboom starter in 1984. Hogeboom looked impressive, leading the Cowboys to a 20–13 win in the opener. However, he stumbled midway through the season, and White regained his job. Still, the Cowboys limped to a 9–7 finish and missed the playoffs.

From 1985 until his last year in 1988, White alternated between being a starter and a backup. As he had done throughout his career, he would make a great play then follow up with a fumble or interception at a critical time. During White's last four seasons, the Cowboys made the playoffs only once, suffering a 20–0 loss to the Los Angeles Rams in the 1985 divisional playoffs.

After he retired, Staubach always cheered for White. He thought Landry made a huge mistake by choosing Hogeboom over White.

"Danny was probably the most underrated player Dallas ever had," Staubach said. "But for some reason that I still don't understand, the team seemed to turn on him."

When Jimmy Johnson took over as coach before the 1989 season, he pressured White to retire. Johnson wanted to develop the quarterback of the future, No. 1 draft choice Troy Aikman. White reluctantly walked away from the game. Soon, he began to fade in fans' memory as Aikman turned in Staubach-like seasons.

Today, Tony Romo has developed into the next great Cowboys' quarterback. White's place in history seems to diminish each year. That's a shame. It's doubtful any quarterback could have followed Staubach and done as well.

18 The Catch

Mention The Catch, and most diehard NFL fans recall the game. The famous play occurred in the NFC Championship Game between the

Cowboys and San Francisco 49ers on January 10, 1982.

Dallas quarterback Danny White had thrown a 21-yard touchdown pass to tight end Doug Cosbie early in the fourth quarter to give the Cowboys a 27–21 lead. With less than five minutes remaining, the 49ers began a drive at their own 11-yard line. Quarterback Joe Montana, who had already thrown three interceptions, began driving the team down the field. He used short passes, draw plays, and even a reverse to keep the drive alive. After 10 plays, Montana had the 49ers at the Cowboys' 6-yard line with less than a minute remaining.

On third down, Montana rolled out to his right, eluding a rush by defensive end Ed "Too Tall" Jones and tackle Larry Bethea. Just as Montana was about to be pressured out of bounds, he lofted a ball high over Jones' outstretched arms. The ball seemed to be too high to reach. Receiver Dwight Clark, who had slipped past Dallas cornerback Everson Walls, leaped high and made a dramatic fingertip catch. His feet came down inches from the back of the end zone.

The play gave San Francisco a 28–27 lead with only 51 seconds left. The Cowboys, however, didn't give up. On first down, White drilled a pass to receiver Drew Pearson across the middle. He broke free and, for a split-second, looked like he might score. However, San Francisco cornerback Eric Wright grabbed just enough of Pearson's jersey to bring him to the ground.

The Cowboys still had time. But on the next play, White fumbled as he dropped back to pass. The 49ers recovered and ran out the clock to win.

"I was stunned," Pearson said. "We never expected the 49ers to be able to drive it like they did and win the game."

The Catch did more than end the Cowboys' 1981 season. It propelled the San Francisco 49ers to the first of four Super Bowl wins in the 1980s. As a result, the 49ers became known as the team of the '80s, while Dallas' fortunes turned south. In 1982, the Cowboys lost again in the NFC Championship Game, 31–17 to the Washington Redskins. They wouldn't win another playoff game the remainder of the decade. Dallas began a steady decline that ended with Tom Landry's ouster as coach following a

3–13 record in 1988. The next year, in Jimmy Johnson's first season, the Cowboys fell further to 1–15.

"The Catch" seemed to curse the Cowboys more than any play in their history.

19 Hail Mary

A Hail Mary pass is a common football expression today. It refers to a long, last-ditch play that a losing team might attempt.

The phrase stems from a 1975 playoff game between the Cowboys and the Minnesota Vikings. The Cowboys met the heavily favored Vikings in a divisional playoff game in frigid Minnesota. Dallas was coming off a surprising 10–4 regular season in what was expected to be a rebuilding year. Minnesota, led by its Purple People Eaters defense, had compiled a stellar 12–2 record.

With less than two minutes left in the game, Dallas trailed the Vikings, 14–10. The Cowboys started a drive on their own 15-yard line. Quarterback Roger Staubach, the master of late comebacks, methodically led the Cowboys down the field. He threw five straight passes to clutch receiver Drew Pearson. The last catch, a critical 22-yarder on fourth down, moved the ball to the 50-yard line with 24 seconds to play.

Staubach lined up five yards behind center in the shotgun formation. Pearson spread out to the right. When the ball was snapped, Pearson streaked down the sideline. Staubach lofted a long pass that was too short. Pearson had to break stride and turn around to look for the ball. As he did, he collided with Vikings cornerback Nate Wright. Wright fell down, and Pearson made the catch after juggling the ball. He then backpedaled five yards into the end zone, to giving Dallas a 17–14 victory. Pearson tossed the ball into the stands in celebration.

The sellout crowd fell silent at the miracle comeback. Wright protested vigorously that Pearson pushed him to make the catch, but officials let the play stand.

"I have never had a more eerie sensation on the football field than during the aftermath of our touchdown," Staubach said. "The crowd was so shocked there wasn't a sound from the stands. It was as though all of a sudden we were playing in an empty stadium."

Pearson still gets asked about the play.

"There was no deliberate push," he said. "Cowboy fans believe me. Viking fans don't."

The Hail Mary pass became the signature play of Pearson's outstanding career from 1973 to 1983. He eclipsed many of the receiving records set by the great Bob Hayes in the 1960s.

Pearson began his career as a skinny free agent out of the University of Tulsa. He had only so-so speed but a big heart and great hands. He quickly bonded with Staubach. The two practiced alone for hours, perfecting their timing. Pearson became Staubach's go-to receiver in the late 1970s.

Pearson's career came to an abrupt end after the 1983 season. He fell asleep at the wheel of his car early one morning and crashed into the back of a parked 18-wheeler. He suffered serious internal injuries, including a lacerated liver. Pearson's younger brother, who was riding with him, died.

Doctors advised Pearson to retire. They said a hard hit could lead to a possibly fatal hemorrhage. Pearson struggled with the decision before deciding a comeback would be too dangerous.

By then, he had secured his place in Cowboys' history. He finished with 489 receptions and 48 touchdowns and was named to three Pro Bowls.

"Drew is very special to me," Staubach said. "There was good chemistry between us. I always felt if I threw the ball out there he'd make the play, which is the highest compliment a quarterback can pay a receiver."

20 Tony Dorsett

Before Cowboy fans cheered Emmitt Smith, they marveled at the magic of Tony Dorsett. Unlike Smith, Dorsett never overpowered tacklers. At only 190 pounds, he couldn't. Dorsett gained yardage with blinding speed and shifty moves that caused defenders to rarely get a clean hit on him.

Dorsett ran by defensive linemen before they even knew he had the ball.

"We've never had a back with this much breakaway ability," coach Tom Landry once said.

The Cowboys chose Dorsett with their No. 1 pick in the 1977 draft, the second choice overall. Dorsett, who won the Heisman Trophy at the University of Pittsburgh, seemed headed for the expansion Seattle Seahawks. They had the right to pick him, because they had compiled the league's worst record the year before.

However, Dorsett didn't want to play for the Seahawks, and the Cowboys desperately needed a big-time back. So Dallas pulled off a major trade, swapping their first-round pick and three second-round choices for Dorsett. It turned out to be a steal.

As a rookie, Dorsett didn't start immediately. Landry brought him along slowly, relying on veteran back Preston Pearson. In the 10th game of the 1977 season, Dorsett finally got his first start. Two weeks later, he rushed for 206 yards in a win over division rival Philadelphia. Dorsett finished the year with 1,007 yards rushing and 13 touchdowns. He was named the NFL Offensive Rookie of the Year.

The Cowboys cruised to a 12–2 record, marched through the playoffs, and crushed the Denver Broncos, 27–10, in Super Bowl XII. Dorsett played a solid game, rushing for 66 yards and scoring a touchdown.

His best season occurred in 1981. Dorsett rushed for 1,646 yards, a team record. He missed the league's rushing title by only 28 yards. In 1986, Dorsett suddenly found himself sharing the limelight with new acquisition

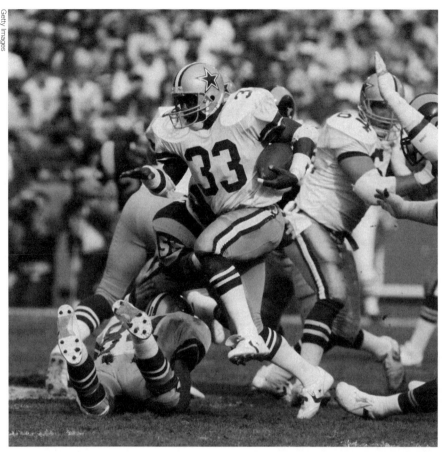

Tony Dorsett runs for daylight during the Cowboys 1985 NFC Divisional Playoff Game against the Los Angeles Rams on January 4, 1986.

Herschel Walker. The Cowboys signed the former Heisman Trophy winner after the upstart United States Football League folded.

Fans and coaches envisioned a Dream Backfield—Dorsett the speedster and Walker the power back. But neither player wanted to share the carries, and they had an uneasy relationship. Dorsett finished the 1986 season with 748 yards, while Walker had 737. But Walker scored 14 touchdowns, compared to only six for Dorsett.

In 1987, Walker clearly became the team's featured back. He rushed for 891 yards, while Dorsett had only 456. Dorsett, then 33, knew he would

41

The Longest Run

Few records in sports can never be broken. Dorsett holds one of them, a 99-yard touchdown run.

It occurred on January 3, 1983, in a game against the Minnesota Vikings. In the fourth quarter, the Cowboys had a first down on their own 1-yard line. Quarterback Danny White handed off to Dorsett, and he burst through the middle.

He stiffed-arm a defender, angled for the sideline and outran everyone to the end zone. Ironically, the Cowboys had only 10 players on the field. Fullback Ron Springs, Dorsett's lead blocker, remained on the sidelines because of a mix-up.

"It was only after I finally got back to the bench that I realized what I had accomplished," Dorsett said. "I had run 99 yards—the longest run from scrimmage in National Football League history."

get even fewer carries the next year. He asked to be traded, and the Cowboys shipped him to the Denver Broncos for a fifth-round draft pick. Dorsett played one year for Denver, rushing for 703 yards. He retired with 12,739 yards, the second-highest total in league history at the time.

During his 12-year career, Dorsett was named to four Pro Bowls. In 1994, he was inducted into the Pro Football Hall of Fame. Smith may have surpassed his records, but no has ever been more exciting to watch than Dorsett.

21 Bob Hayes

Bob Hayes changed the NFL forever. Hayes, an Olympic gold-medal sprinter, brought unprecedented speed to the league when he arrived as a rookie wide receiver in 1965. Until then, defensive secondaries played man-to-man coverage.

Hayes had such blazing speed that defenders couldn't cover him one-on-one. As a result, opposing teams began playing zone defense, in which defensive backs were responsible for an area on the field. As Hayes sped through the secondary, different defenders tried to cover him, often unsuccessfully.

"I doubt there has ever been anyone who revolutionized the offensive game the way Bobby did," Cowboys quarterback Don Meredith said.

The Cowboys drafted Hayes, 5' 11" and 187 pounds, in the seventh round in 1964. He played at Florida A&M University, a historically black college. His biggest claim to fame was winning two gold medals in the 1964 Olympics, one in the 100-meter dash and another anchoring the 400-meter relay. Hayes held the world record of 9.1 seconds in the 100-yard dash, earning him the nickname of World's Fastest Human.

When Hayes joined the Cowboys in 1965, he quickly picked up another nickname: Bullet Bob. He wowed coaches and teammates with his blinding speed, as well as his ability to catch the ball.

"I'd never been a big proponent of track men who played football," coach Tom Landry said. "But Bobby turned out to be a football player who happened to have run track."

In his first game as a rookie, Hayes made an immediate impact. He caught eight passes and scored a touchdown on a 45-yard run. He finished the 1965 season with 12 touchdowns receiving and a 21.8-yard-per-catch average. He earned All-Pro honors and helped the Cowboys achieve a 7–7 record, their first season to reach .500.

In 1966, Hayes set a Cowboys' single-game record with nine catches for 246 yards against the Washington Redskins. Defenders had to be wary of the inevitable Meredith-to-Hayes bomb. During his 10-year career with Dallas, Hayes scored touchdowns of 95, 89, and 85 yards. In one game in 1970, he had four touchdowns.

In the early 1970s, Hayes' career declined, in part, because he didn't adjust well to zone defenses. In addition, defenses began using bump-and-run coverage on Hayes. That meant hitting him on the line to disrupt his pattern. This tactic further offset his huge speed advantage.

In 1974, Hayes lost his starting job to Golden Richards, a second-round pick the previous year. In 1975, the Cowboys traded Hayes to the San Francisco 49ers, and his career ended quickly. Hayes had only six catches before the 49ers released him at mid-season. No other team claimed him.

Hayes' personal life also hit bottom. In 1978, he was convicted on drug delivery charges and spent almost 10 months in state prison. He maintained his innocence. An appeals court later overturned his conviction on a technicality, improper wording in his indictments.

"Going from the penthouse to rock bottom is hard to accept," Hayes said in a prison interview.

Hayes has never made it into the Pro Football Hall of Fame. Many people feel his omission is a travesty because of his lasting impact on the game. In 2001, Hayes was honored with induction into the Cowboys' Ring of Honor. He died the next year from prostate cancer at the age of 59.

"I only played against him in practice," said Cowboys defensive back Mel Renfro, "but Bob Hayes was the only receiver I ever feared."

22 Hollywood Henderson

The Cowboys have had many great players, but they've never had a better all-around athlete than Thomas "Hollywood" Henderson. Henderson, an outside linebacker from 1975 to 1979, had the speed of a wide receiver, the agility of a running back, and the strength of a lineman. His career was cut short by drug problems, poor work habits, and run-ins with coach Tom Landry.

Landry, exasperated with Henderson's me-first attitude, cut him toward the end of the 1979 season. The flamboyant Henderson had mugged for the camera in the closing minutes of a key loss to Washington.

The Cowboys drafted Henderson, 6' 2" and 221 pounds, with their No. 1 pick in 1975. He played at tiny Langston University in central Oklahoma and wasn't widely known by NFL scouts. He turned out to be one of the Cowboys' greatest small-college finds. As a rookie, Henderson was a backup, but he showed his incredible athleticism on special teams.

In only his second game, he returned a kickoff 97 yards for a touchdown. To punctuate the play, he dunked the ball over the goal posts. In his third game as a starter in 1977, Henderson intercepted a pass and returned it 79 yards for a touchdown. Again, he dunked the ball.

In January 1979, the Cowboys met the Pittsburgh Steelers in Super Bowl XIII. Leading up to the game, Henderson shot off his mouth, as was his tendency. He said Steelers' quarterback Terry Bradshaw was so dumb he "couldn't spell 'cat' if you spotted him c and t."

Bradshaw responded with an MVP performance in leading the Steelers to a 35–31 win. After the game, Bradshaw directed a comment at the loud-mouthed linebacker. "Ask Henderson if I was dumb today," he said.

Landry, a rigid disciplinarian, never appreciated Henderson's free-spirited ways. Defensive back Charlie Waters recalls a time when the team was watching a game film. Landry noticed that Henderson was wearing sunglasses even though the lights were out.

"Can you explain why you have sunglasses on in the dark?" Landry asked.

"Coach, when you are cool, the sun's always shining on you," Henderson replied, smiling.

Landry turned and walked away.

Waters said he liked Henderson, although he, too, grew frustrated with his antics.

"He was so athletic, so strong and bright that pro football came easy to him," Waters said. "He was full of confidence. Thomas also had an engaging personality. He could charm the fangs off a snake, and he had an infectious smile. He was a mess, but he was a treat to play with."

By 1979, Henderson had become a distraction to the team. He missed meetings and practices, and his game performances slipped. In the 12th game of the season, the Cowboys lost 34–20 to their biggest rival, the Washington Redskins. Instead of taking the loss seriously, as other players were, Henderson clowned for the cameras on the sidelines. The next day, Landry cut him.

The San Francisco 49ers signed Henderson and then released him. So did the Houston Oilers and the Miami Dolphins. In 1981, at the age of only 28, Hollywood Henderson's NFL career was over. "Thomas could have been a dominating force in this league," general manager Tex Schramm said.

After football, Henderson's life spiraled downward. In 1984, he was convicted of having sex with a minor and served more than two years in prison. After his release in 1987, he wrote *Out of Control: Confessions of an NFL Casualty*. He detailed his drug use and wild behavior.

"Today, I live one day at a time," he wrote. "I've made a lot of battlefield mistakes…I'm lucky to be alive."

23 Duane Thomas

Emmitt Smith and Tony Dorsett were the greatest running backs in Cowboy history. But another back, Duane Thomas, may have had even more talent. Sadly, it went largely unrealized in a brief, troubled two-year career. The Cowboys made Thomas their No. 1 draft choice in 1970 out of West Texas State University.

At 6' 2" and 220 pounds, Thomas had size and outstanding speed. He showed his immense talent early. In the sixth game of his rookie year, Thomas replaced the injured starter, Calvin Hill. Thomas responded with 134 yards rushing, including a 47-yard touchdown run. He proved the performance wasn't a fluke. Thomas finished the 1970 season with 803 yards rushing and an average of 5.3 yards per carry—the league's best average. He received Rookie of the Year honors.

The Cowboys met the Baltimore Colts in Super Bowl V at the end of Thomas' rookie year. He had one of his worst games. He rushed for only 35 yards and had a critical fumble that probably cost the Cowboys the game. The Cowboys were leading 13–6 in the third quarter, and had the ball on the Baltimore 2-yard line.

Thomas took a handoff and plowed to within inches of the goal line before fumbling. A mad scramble for the ball ensued. Dallas center Dave Manders leaped from the pile of players, holding the ball high for the referees to see.

The officials inexplicably awarded the ball to the Colts. They seized the momentum and scored to tie the game. Then, on the game's last play, the Colts kicked a 32-yard field goal to win, 16–13.

After his standout rookie year, Thomas held out for a new contract. He called a press conference during training camp and lambasted coach Tom Landry, general manager Tex Schramm, and personnel director Gil Brandt.

The Cowboys, worn out with Thomas, traded him to the New England Patriots. But the Patriots voided the trade because Thomas wouldn't take a physical or follow instructions during practice. He wound up back with the Cowboys but continued his contract holdout. In the second game of the 1971 season, however, he announced he'd play under protest.

"The only reason I'm coming back is for my people, the black people," he said.

He may have been ready to play, but he wasn't ready to talk to reporters or teammates. "It was amazing," said defensive tackle Jethro Pugh. "We were best friends, but you could ask him something and he was just silent."

Despite his surliness, Thomas played well and led the team in rushing with 793 yards. The Cowboys rolled to an 11–3 record and advanced to the Super Bowl for the second straight year. Thomas rushed for 95 yards and scored a touchdown to help Dallas thump the Miami Dolphins, 24–3.

In the locker room after the game, Thomas again demonstrated his enigmatic behavior.

"Are you really that fast?" a television announcer asked him.

"Evidently," Thomas replied.

"Your weight fluctuates," the announcer said, again trying to elicit a response.

"I weigh what I need to," Thomas said flatly.

During the 1972 training camp, he continued his silent treatment and skipped practices without explanation. Landry tried to tolerate Thomas, but finally had enough. The Cowboys traded him to the San Diego Chargers.

"There's no telling how many hours and days and weeks and months Tom spent on Duane, trying to straighten him out," fullback Walt Garrison said. "He wanted to get Duane back on the right track. But it didn't work."

After being traded to the Chargers, Thomas held out the entire year in a contract dispute. In 1973, he was traded to the Washington Redskins, but couldn't break into the starting lineup. He spent another season with the Redskins then signed with the upstart World Football League. The league folded within two months of his signing. In 1976, Thomas asked the Cowboys for another shot.

His attitude wasn't a problem, but his talent was. He had lost speed and was cut before the start of the 1976 season. He tried and failed with the Green Bay Packers, too.

"I'll always have a lot of regrets about Duane," Schramm said. "He obviously had a lot of ability and proved it, but just for two years. That's tragic."

24 Don Meredith

The Cowboys needed a talented young quarterback in their early days as an expansion team. They found one in Don Meredith. A two-time All American at Southern Methodist University, Meredith joined the Cowboys in their inaugural 1960 season. He had the size, arm, and charisma to become a star.

Coach Tom Landry brought Meredith along slowly. Veteran Eddie LeBaron started most of the games between 1960 and 1962, before Meredith took over in 1963. Those were lean years. The Cowboys never won more than five games in a season.

In 1965, Meredith and the team began to improve. The Cowboys finished 7–7 for their first non-losing season. In 1966, Meredith had his best year, completing 52 percent of his passes and throwing 24 touchdowns. He was named NFL Player of the Year. The Cowboys compiled a 10–3–1 record and faced off against the powerful Green Bay Packers in the NFL Championship.

Meredith had only a so-so game, but he kept the Cowboys within striking distance. With two minutes remaining in the game, he had led the Cowboys to the Green Bay 2-yard line. Dallas trailed, 34–27. The Cowboys couldn't score on first, second, or third down. On fourth down, with the game on the line, Meredith threw an interception in the end zone, and the Packers held on to win.

The Cowboys earned a rematch with the Packers in the 1967 NFL

Getty Images

The colorful but cowboy-tough Don Meredith warms up on the sidelines prior to a 1966 game.

Championship Game, but they again fell short, 21–17. Meredith had a dismal game in the frigid Ice Bowl, completing only 10 of 25 passes for 59 yards.

Dallas fans rarely gave Meredith the credit he deserved. He played through a string of injuries, including cracked ribs, a broken nose, and a twisted knee. He had some great games, but fans seemed to focus on his bad ones. Many blamed him for the team's failure to win a championship.

"Don Meredith was outstanding," Landry said. "He was one of our toughest players ever. Sometimes I don't think the fans realized what he was sacrificing, the pain he was playing in."

In 1968, fans and players had high expectations for the Cowboys. Meredith had a stellar season, throwing 21 touchdowns, but the team bowed out in an early playoff upset. Again, fans booed Meredith. At the end of the season, tired of the criticism and nagging injuries, Meredith retired. He was only 31 years old.

Throughout his career, Meredith struggled to get along with Landry. Meredith liked to party, and his easygoing personality clashed with the intense, disciplined Landry. His teammates, however, loved Meredith.

"He didn't have an exceptional arm, and he was erratic," receiver Pete Gent said. "But he had the amazing ability to coalesce everyone around him. Everyone wanted to win for him."

After retiring, Meredith quickly became a successful broadcaster. He was part of the original crew of ABC's *Monday Night Football* in 1970, and remained with the broadcast off and on until 1984. Dandy Don's folksy style and humor made him a bigger star as an announcer than he'd ever been as a player.

Since leaving *Monday Night Football*, Meredith has kept a low profile. He lives in Santa Fe, New Mexico, and refuses most interview requests. "I don't miss the limelight," he said.

The Cowboys, however, have never forgotten his contributions. In 1976, he became one of the first players inducted into the Ring of Honor at Texas Stadium.

"I'm very sorry he didn't stay around long enough to win a Super Bowl," general manager Tex Schramm said. "He deserved that and would have been recognized as one of the very best."

25 America's Team

The Cowboys have more of a national following than any other NFL team. So it shouldn't be surprising that they've earned the nickname of America's Team. But the label has been both a blessing and a curse. It's given the Cowboys a higher national profile, but it's also set them up as an enticing target for opponents.

The term America's Team was first used in 1978 by an editor at NFL Films. He was producing an annual highlight film for the Cowboys, and he was searching for a title. He hit on America's Team because he realized that the Cowboys had fans all over the country. Dallas players received a private showing of the film before it was released to the public, and they were told of the name.

"We were labeled 'America's Team,' and the narrator said something about the Cowboys being the Notre Dame of professional football," quarterback Roger Staubach said. "I thought it was a joke, and they'd bring in the real highlight film next."

It was no joke.

Cowboys' general manager Tex Schramm was perhaps the only member of the organization who liked the nickname. He was a consummate marketer, and he saw the public relations value in being called America's Team. However, most players and coaches cringed at the nickname. They thought it sounded presumptuous and would give opposing teams extra motivation to beat them, and they were right.

"I think that title gave us a lot more trouble than it was worth," coach Tom Landry said. "I don't know anyone on the Cowboys who liked that label to start with."

Staubach said opponents used to taunt the Cowboys, calling them America's Team. "Every time we lost, somebody on the other team always mentioned it," he said.

Cowboy Haters

The Cowboys have plenty of detractors to go with their legion of admirers. Some people can't stomach the America's Team tag. They think the Cowboys have an unwarranted good guy image and receive over-adoring media coverage. After all, the Cowboys have had just as many players run afoul of the law as any other team.

Detractors aren't shy about expressing their feelings. Consider the books that have been written: *The Semi-Official Dallas Cowboys Haters' Handbook; Mamas, Don't Let Your Cowboys Grow Up to be Babies*, and *I Hate the Dallas Cowboys and Who Elected Them America's Team Anyway?*

"Every time I hear the Dallas Cowboys referred to as America's Team, I feel like tossing my cookies—preferably somewhere in the direction of Dallas," writes Burt Sugar, editor of *I Hate the Cowboys*.

Sugar had 20 sportswriters and former NFL players tell why they hate the Cowboys. Phil Villapiano, a linebacker for the Oakland Raiders, said the Raiders would never have embraced a nickname like America's Team.

"'America's Meanest Team,' probably," Villapiano wrote. "'America's Greatest Team,' definitely. But 'America's Team'? That crap would never have worked in Oakland."

America's Team, like any nickname, stuck because it rang true. Cowboy games then and now draw huge national TV audiences. No other NFL team generates as much revenue from licensed merchandise, such as shirts, hats, and bumper stickers.

The Cowboys' winning tradition helps explain their popularity. So does the steady stream of high-profile players starting with Don Meredith and Bob Lilly in the 1960s, and continuing with Staubach, Drew Pearson, Tony Dorsett, Troy Aikman, Emmitt Smith, Michael Irvin, and—most recently—Tony Romo and Terrell Owens.

These players, and many others, had personality and pizzazz to go along with great talent. Fans wanted to follow their exploits on and off the field. Even when the Cowboys have had losing spells, such as in the 1980s, they've never lost their devoted fan base. Supporters seemed to know that the 'Boys will eventually be back.

Today's team proves the point. The Romo-led Cowboys are an offensive juggernaut complemented by a rock-solid defense. Plus, there's the always-enticing storyline of Romo's personal life.

It's difficult not to follow the Cowboys.

26 Cliff Harris and Charlie Waters

In 1970, Cliff Harris and Charlie Waters joined the Cowboys. They quickly became best friends, even though they initially competed for the same starting spot. Eventually, they both earned starting roles and developed into two of the best defensive backs in the league.

The two took dramatically different routes to the Cowboys. Harris made the team as a free agent out of tiny Ouachita Baptist University in Arkansas. Waters, on the other hand, was a third-round draft pick from a big school, Clemson.

As rookies, they both played free safety. Harris beat out Waters for the starting job and made an immediate impact with his hard-nose tackling. Harris had to miss several games in the second half of the 1970 season because of military service. While he was gone, Waters stepped in and also played well. He intercepted five passes and started in Super Bowl V.

In '71, Harris rejoined the team after completing his military commitment. He bumped Waters from the starting lineup and earned the nickname Captain Crash for his kamikaze-style play.

"He only knows how to play at one speed, and that's full speed," coach Tom Landry said.

Harris, 6' and 190 pounds, made the Pro Bowl every year from 1974 until he retired in 1979. He had several key interceptions, including ones in the 1975 and 1978 NFC Championship games.

"Captain Crash made an impression on every receiver he played against," Waters said. "Before running their routes or locating the ball, the receivers' No. 1 priority for survival was to locate and stay clear of Cliff—

that is, if they wanted to continue playing that day."

In 1972, Waters became a starter at cornerback and remained there until 1974. Those three years were tough for Waters. He lacked the speed of many cornerbacks, and receivers often burned him deep. "If you learn by mistakes, I ought to be a genius," Waters once said.

In 1975, following the retirement of All-Pro Cornell Green, the Cowboys moved Waters to safety to play next to Harris, the other safety. Waters, 6' 1" and 195 pounds, finally found a home. At safety, he didn't have as many man-to-man pass coverage responsibilities, and he focused on making tackles. Waters earned All-Pro honors from 1976 to 1978.

In 1979, he suffered a major knee injury in a preseason game and missed the entire year. After surgery and a lengthy rehabilitation, Waters returned in 1980. He had to wear a brace and had lost much of his quickness and agility. He finished his career in 1981 as a player-coach. He helped develop a young secondary that included free agents Everson Walls and Michael Downs.

Waters retired with 41 interceptions, not including nine in the playoffs. He also started in five Super Bowls.

"Charlie and I had a unique bond," Harris said. "Though we were very competitive with each other, we worked together very well, like no tandem on the Cowboys ever has. I truly felt that Charlie, at times, knew what I was thinking."

Waters played two years longer, but Harris made more of an impact on the game. Unlike previous safeties, he didn't simply remain deep in the secondary and try to prevent long passes. He rushed to the line of scrimmage and made key tackles like a linebacker.

"Cliff changed the way free safeties play the position," Staubach said. "I think he's Hall of Fame material because of it."

Many others agree. Harris, however, has never made it into the Pro Football Hall of Fame and may not. Two decades have passed since he retired. Harris was honored in 2004 with induction into the Cowboys Ring of Honor at Texas Stadium.

Defensive tackle Randy White, a member of the Hall of Fame and the

Ring of Honor, said Harris played with an intensity that few could match.

"Cliff was a 110-percent guy," White said. "He had no regard for his body. He would knock your head off."

27 Super Bowl XXVIII—Another Rout

After the Cowboys demolished Buffalo in Super Bowl XXVII, people wondered whether they would be a one-hit wonder. Sure, they overwhelmed the Bills, 52–17, but could they stay on top?

Super Bowl XXVIII, a rematch with the Bills, answered any questions. The Cowboys thumped the Bills, 30–13, for the second of three Super Bowl wins in the 1990s. A dynasty was developing.

Even though the final score was lopsided, Dallas struggled early in Super Bowl XXVIII. The Bills outscored the Cowboys 13–6 in the first half. Buffalo's Thurman Thomas ran four yards for a touchdown, and the Bills added two field goals, including a 54-yarder. Dallas could only manage two Eddie Murray field goals.

Early in the third quarter, the Cowboys took control of the game. Defensive tackle Leon Lett stripped the ball from Thomas, and safety James Washington picked it up and ran 46 yards for a touchdown. The game was now tied, 13–13.

Dallas soon got the ball back. Emmitt Smith, playing with a separated shoulder, showed the courage that would make him the NFL's all-time leading rusher. He carried the ball on seven plays of an eight-play, 64-yard drive. He capped it with a 15-yard touchdown run to give Dallas a 20–13 lead.

"I love watching that drive," Smith said. "Normally, I don't watch myself in old games. But I put that Super Bowl drive in my VCR a lot. I'll never forget it as long as I live."

Buffalo fought back, but Washington made another huge play, intercepting a pass to kill a drive. Smith scored another touchdown on a 1-yard run early in the fourth quarter, and Murray tacked on a third field goal late to make the final score 30–13.

The Cowboys showed their dominance on both sides of the ball. The defense shut down the Bills, limiting them to only 87 yards rushing. Smith ran for more than that himself, picking up 132 yards. He was named Most Valuable Player. With the award, Smith became the first player to win an NFL rushing title and be selected Super Bowl MVP in the same year.

Washington came in a close second in the MVP voting, thanks to his fumble return for a TD and interception. He also added 11 tackles. Washington said he was hoping he and Smith could share the MVP award, as Randy White and Harvey Martin had done back in Super Bowl XII.

"I had some big hits that changed the tempo of the game," Washington said.

The win was even sweeter considering how the 1993 season began. Smith held out the first two games in a bitter contract dispute with owner Jerry Jones. The Cowboys lost both games. The public largely sided with Smith and began calling for Jones to meet his contract demands. Four days after the second loss, Jones made Smith an acceptable offer: a four-year, $13.6 million contract.

With Smith back in the lineup, the Cowboys quickly returned to top form. They won seven-straight games and got on a roll that culminated in another world championship. By the end of the season, the Smith-Jones feud was long forgotten.

"Our second Super Bowl victory confirmed for me that we were a balanced organization that could deal with all sorts of circumstances," Jones said.

28 Jimmy Fired

You would think back-to-back Super Bowl wins would engender harmony between the coach and owner. Wrong, at least in the case of the Dallas Cowboys. Even though the Cowboys hammered the Buffalo Bills

Few could have predicted that just a few months after this photo was taken, following the Cowboys' win in Super Bowl XXVIII in Atlanta on January 30, 1994, that Jimmy Johnson and Jerry Jones would part ways.

in Super Bowls XXVII and XXVIII, owner Jerry Jones and head coach Jimmy Johnson feuded.

Each man wanted more of the credit for the Cowboys' amazing transformation from a 1–15 team to world champion. Actually, both played critical roles. Jones provided the financial backing to sign top players. Johnson provided the football savvy to bring out the best in them.

Publicly, the two gave no indication of a problem. But behind the scenes, tension had been building between Jones and Johnson for more than a year. Their dysfunctional relationship came to an abrupt end less than two months after Super Bowl XXVIII. At an NFL meeting on March 23, 1994,

Jones walked over to a table where Johnson and some friends were gathered. They were celebrating the Cowboys' success.

Jones proposed a toast.

"Here's to the Dallas Cowboys, and here's to the people who made it possible to win two Super Bowls!" he said proudly.

No one at the table, including Johnson, joined in the toast. Jones tried again but got the same silent response. Jones didn't like being ignored.

"Go on with your [bleeping] party," he said, storming off.

Shortly after midnight, Jones sat in a hotel bar with some Dallas sportswriters and dropped a bombshell. He planned to fire Johnson. Jones skewered Johnson, calling him a disloyal SOB. Then he delivered the ultimate insult to Johnson.

"I think there are 500 coaches who could have coached this team to the Super Bowl," Jones told reporters.

Johnson, when he heard of the comments, flew into a rage. He immediately packed his bags and left the Orlando meeting. When he calmed down a little, he talked to the press.

"I know I'm arrogant," Johnson said. "I know I'm self-serving. But somebody please tell me what I've done ... so wrong to be ripped the way I have? To my mind, I just got to the pinnacle of my profession."

The public mudslinging stunned and angered players, many of whom sided with Johnson.

"I don't understand popping off like that," Emmitt Smith said of the owner. "I think Jerry is trying to stir up controversy because the man can't live straight unless there is controversy in his life."

After the blowup, Jones and Johnson held several awkward meetings. They tried to find a way to co-exist for one more season in hopes of winning an unprecedented third straight Super Bowl. But, finally, they realized their relationship was so damaged it couldn't be fixed.

On March 29, 1994, six days after Jones' verbal attack on Johnson, the two held a news conference to announce the split. They each put on a happy face and had only kind words for the other.

"It's fantastic what we were able to do," Johnson said to the press. "And when I say 'we,' I mean 'we.' I appreciate what he's done for me."

Johnson immediately had several offers to coach other teams. He turned them down and went to work as a television analyst. After being out of football two years, Johnson became coach of the Miami Dolphins in 1996. His four-year tenure, unlike his stint in Dallas, was largely unsuccessful. Johnson compiled a 36–28 regular-season record. He won two playoff games, but never took the Dolphins to the Super Bowl.

In the years since the Jones-Johnson divorce, both have admitted mistakes. Jones regrets saying that 500 coaches could have won two Super Bowls with the Cowboys.

"That was a mistake," Jones said. "But I felt strongly about the personnel of the team we had put together."

It's impossible to say who deserves more of the blame for their split. But this much is clear—the team suffered as a result. Many agree with an assessment by Joe Brodsky, the Cowboys' running back coach in the 1990s.

"We probably would have won three or four Super Bowls if Jimmy and Jerry could have found a way to work together," he said.

29 Barry Hired

Barry Switzer seemed like an unlikely choice to coach the Dallas Cowboys in 1994. First, he had never coached in the NFL, even as an assistant. Second, Switzer had been away from football for five years.

He had made his mark as a college coach. In 16 years at the University of Oklahoma, Switzer won three national championships, the last in 1985. He compiled a remarkable 157–29–4 record. But in 1989, despite all his success, school officials pushed him out because of off-the-field incidents by players.

One player shot a teammate, one was convicted of selling cocaine, and two were convicted of raping a female student.

Switzer's coaching career seemed over until he received a call from an old friend, Jerry Jones, in March 1994. The Cowboys' owner made Switzer an incredible offer: How would he like to coach the team?

"I said, 'Who wouldn't want to coach the best team with the best coaching staff and the best players?'" Switzer recalled.

Jones dismissed criticism that Switzer would be ill suited for the job. He didn't care that Switzer ran the Wishbone offense in college, instead of a pro-style passing game.

"Barry is recognized as a motivator, and he's loyal to his players to a fault," Jones said. "Those were the traits I wanted in my head coach."

Jones and Switzer held a press conference to announce the hiring. Switzer could hardly contain his excitement.

"Get ready to watch the Dallas Cowboys be the best team in the NFL," he shouted. "We got a job to do and we're going to do it, baby!"

Jones and Switzer had a long history together. Switzer was an assistant coach at the University of Arkansas in 1964 when Jones played for the Razorbacks. Still, many Dallas fans didn't embrace Switzer. They viewed him as the enemy from his days as OU's coach. Switzer's Sooners would often beat the Texas Longhorns in their annual game.

Players had doubts, too. Switzer's friendly, easygoing approach contrasted with Johnson's drill sergeant mentality. Switzer was a tough sell around the league as well. Former San Francisco 49ers coach Bill Walsh echoed many people's thoughts when he called Switzer a "ceremonial coach." Walsh predicted that Jones would really call the shots.

The uncertainty about Switzer created great anticipation about the 1994 season. In the opener, the Cowboys dominated the Pittsburgh Steelers, 26–9. They also won the second week 20–17, over the Houston Oilers. After losing the third game in overtime, Dallas chalked up six straight wins. They were on their way to a 12–4 record and a divisional title.

In the first playoff game, the Cowboys whipped the Green Bay Packers, 35–9. But they lost to San Francisco, 38–28, in the NFC Championship Game, missing a chance to win a third straight Super Bowl. Many people thought the Cowboys would have beaten the 49ers and won a third title if Johnson had still been coach.

Jones acknowledged the talk. "I think there definitely will be speculation as to what we could have done out there if Jimmy were the coach," he said.

In Switzer's second year, the Cowboys finished 12–4 again and won a fourth-straight NFC East title. They swept through the playoffs, beating the Philadelphia and Green Bay, to meet the Pittsburgh Steelers in Super Bowl XXX. Switzer knew he faced pressure to win.

"If I don't win, I'm a failure," he said.

Switzer and the team didn't fail. Dallas won, 27–17, and the Cowboys became the first team to win three Super Bowls in four years. Switzer and Jones held the Lombardi Trophy together after the game and embraced.

"We did it our way, baby!" Switzer screamed.

Switzer's third season in 1996 was less memorable. The Cowboys dipped to 10–6, and lost in the second round of the playoffs. In 1997, their slide continued. By this point, the Cowboys had lost many starters from the Super Bowls to free agency. They hadn't drafted well, and the results were beginning to show. The Cowboys ended the 1997 season with five straight losses for an unthinkable 6–10 record.

"This didn't happen overnight," Aikman said accurately. "We've been declining the last couple of years to where we are now."

Jones blamed Switzer. He fired him with one year remaining on his contract. The owner couldn't tolerate how far the Cowboys had fallen.

"We can't let that happen again," he said.

30 Visit Texas Stadium

Watching the Cowboys on television is okay most of the time, but a true fan occasionally needs to see the team in person. Tickets are expensive, and traffic is a hassle. But there's no substitute for hearing the hits and seeing the plays unfold in person.

It's an entirely different experience than you get watching the game at home. For almost 30 years, the Cowboys have played at Texas Stadium in the Dallas suburb of Irving. But you'd better hurry if you want to see the Cowboys play there. The 2008 season is the Cowboys' last at Texas Stadium before they move to a new $1 billion stadium in Arlington, another Dallas suburb.

Texas Stadium opened in 1971 at a cost of $35 million. It's most famous for its large rectangular hole in the roof. The idea was to shield fans from the elements while letting the game be played outside. Jerry Jones, who bought the team in 1989, talked of closing the hole and expanding the stadium early on, but rejected the idea as too costly and impractical.

Texas Stadium seats only about 65,000, making it too small to host a Super Bowl. Jones has already landed a Super Bowl at the new stadium, which can seat up to 100,000. Texas Stadium was one of the first venues to have luxury suites, a staple of modern stadiums. It had only 16 at first, and they sold for the then-princely sum of $50,000. Today, annual leases for the suites range from $40,000 to $125,000, according to the team's official website, www.dallascowboys.com.

If you want to sit in the stands, expect to pay between $75 and $140. For an extra $10, you can get admission to the Stadium Club overlooking the field. There, you can eat a lunch buffet for another $50. Jones has devised all kinds of ways to get your money.

Before or after the game, you can visit the Corral, a tent outside the stadium that has food, drinks, and live music. The current admission is $5, and you must have a game ticket. If you like to tailgate, you'll have plenty of company in the parking lot.

The Cowboys offer tours of Texas Stadium and will book private parties and corporate events. When the Cowboys aren't playing, high school football games, concerts, motorcycle races, and other events are held.

If you go to Texas Stadium, be sure to see the nine-foot-tall bronze statue of former coach Tom Landry outside Gate 1. It was unveiled on April 11, 2001, to honor Landry, who died in 2000 of leukemia. The legendary Landry coached the Cowboys from their first season in 1960 until 1989, when Jones bought the team and fired him. For years, Landry was affectionately known as The Only Coach the Cowboys Have Ever Had.

Texas Stadium replaced the Cotton Bowl as the Cowboys' home, and the fan base changed when they moved. The aging Cotton Bowl is located on the state fairgrounds near downtown Dallas. Tickets at that venue were affordable, and the Cowboys tended to draw a working-class crowd.

Not so at Texas Stadium. Ticket prices shot through the hole in the roof when the Cowboys moved there, excluding many regular Joes. As a result, the crowd became noticeably more affluent.

Duane Thomas, the Cowboys' talented but enigmatic running back, scored the first touchdown at Texas Stadium on October 24, 1971. His 56-yard run helped Dallas beat the New England Patriots, 44–21. Since then, Cowboy legends from Drew Pearson to Troy Aikman have played their entire careers at Texas Stadium.

Fans witnessed a historic moment on October 27, 2002, when Emmitt Smith became the NFL's all-time leading rusher. He surpassed Walter Payton's record of 16,726 yards on an 11-yard run against the Seattle Seahawks. Smith played four more games at Texas Stadium before ending his Dallas career. He signed with the Arizona Cardinals for his final two seasons.

The new Cowboys stadium, undoubtedly, will host many unforgettable moments. But any facility would be hard-pressed to top the excitement and drama that's occurred at Texas Stadium.

31 Bill Bates

Bill Bates came to the Cowboys as a free agent in 1983. He retired in 1997 as one of the most beloved players in team history. Bates defined hustle. He made the team because of his kamikaze style on special teams. He remained on the team because of his versatility. During his lengthy career, he played cornerback, safety, and linebacker.

Bates, 6' 1" and 200 pounds, attended the University of Tennessee.

The hard-working, hard-charging Bill Bates, shown here during a November 1995 game, was a fan favorite in Big D.

Despite having an outstanding college career, Bates attracted little interest from NFL scouts because he was considered slow. Only two teams, the Cowboys and the Seattle Seahawks, offered Bates a free agent contract. It was an easy choice. Bates had been a Cowboys fan since childhood.

At training camp, Bates immediately impressed team officials with his hustle and intensity.

"People would look at him and say he wasn't fast enough," said Gil Brandt, former player personnel director. "But he worked hard, and he stuck."

He particularly excelled on special teams. Week after week, Bates would tear down the field on kickoffs or punts, sidestep or run through blockers, and make a big hit on the ball carrier. Television announcers began commenting on this madman who wore No. 40. As a rookie, Bates was named the NFL's Special Teams Player of the Year. He won the award again his next year. Several years later, his scrappy play persuaded NFL officials to create a special teams slot on the Pro Bowl.

In 1986, Bates's fourth season, he finally earned a starting spot at strong safety. He kept it for three years. He had his best season in 1988 with 124 tackles.

When Jimmy Johnson became coach in 1989, Bates's future didn't look bright. Johnson put a premium on speed. He wanted fast players, and Bates wasn't fast.

However, Bates impressed Johnson with his intensity and dedication and remained on the team. Under Johnson, Bates didn't start, but he played regularly on special teams and in passing situations.

In 1992, Bates suffered a serious knee injury and had season-ending surgery. The injury snapped Bates's string of playing in 79 consecutive games. While he was out, Bates helped coach the special teams. That season, the Cowboys made it to their first Super Bowl in 15 years. They demolished the Buffalo Bills, 52–17, in Super Bowl XXVII. Bates, who deserved to play in the game as much as anyone, had to watch from the sidelines.

In the off-season, Bates underwent a lengthy rehabilitation period. He had suffered a torn anterior cruciate ligament (ACL), one of the most serious injuries. Some players never return, but Bates did. In 1993, he led the special teams with 25 tackles and helped the Cowboys return to the

Super Bowl. Bates played on passing downs in the 30–13 whipping of Buffalo in Super Bowl XXVIII.

In 1995, Bates and his teammates won a third Super Bowl in four years. The Cowboys whipped the Pittsburgh Steelers, 27–17, in Super Bowl XXX. Two years later, Bates reluctantly retired. Owner Jerry Jones and new coach Chan Gailey urged him to step down and become an assistant coach.

"I want to play," Bates said at an emotional press conference. "But I'm focusing on helping this team win as a coach."

During his remarkable 15-year career, Bates played in 217 games. Only defensive end Ed "Too Tall" Jones played in more games, 224. Not bad for a guy nobody bothered to draft.

32 Everson Walls

Everson Walls never lacked confidence. As free agent out of Grambling in 1981, he not only made the Cowboys, he also earned a starting spot at cornerback and led the league in interceptions—the first rookie to do so in 14 years.

How's that for a player no NFL team wanted to draft?

Walls proved that his first year was no fluke. From 1982 to 1985, he had a total of 23 interceptions and made All-Pro every year.

Walls had a knack for making interceptions in college, too. As a senior, he led the country in interceptions with 11. So why wasn't Walls a top draft choice? NFL scouts thought he was too slow, and they questioned the competition he faced at Grambling, a small, historically black college.

But Walls was used to beating the odds. When he graduated from high school in Dallas, no college offered him a scholarship. He walked on at Grambling, made the team and started as a freshman. The same confidence he displayed in college, he brought to the pros.

Walls always wanted to play for the Cowboys. He grew up only two miles from their workout facilities and used to watch them practice. When he arrived for his first training camp in 1981, he immediately impressed coaches with his coverage abilities. He also made big plays. In preseason, he had three interceptions, a fumble recovery, and a blocked punt that he retired for a touchdown. The Cowboys knew they had a playmaker and welcomed him onto the roster.

"People didn't draft him because he didn't have top speed," said Gil Brandt, former Cowboys personnel director. "But he had a great understanding of how to play the game."

In his rookie year, Walls helped the Cowboys advance to the NFC Championship Game against the San Francisco 49ers. He played well, intercepting two passes and recovering a fumble. But he'll always be remembered for being involved in The Catch, a 6-yard touchdown grab by receiver Dwight Clark that won the game for San Francisco. Clark beat Walls in the end zone and leaped high for the pass from Joe Montana. He made the catch with less than a minute remaining to give the 49ers a 28–27 win and a ticket to Super Bowl XVI.

Aside from that one play, Walls turned in a great performance.

"My thoughts of that game have always been mixed feelings because I was on my way to an MVP game," Walls said. "No one ever mentions that part of it."

In 1989, Jimmy Johnson took over as Cowboys' coach and wanted to bring in younger, faster players. He kept Walls for a year, then cut him before the 1990 season. "Everson Walls was a helluva cornerback in his prime," Johnson said. "But in the fall of 1989, he was past his prime."

During his nine-year career with the Cowboys, Walls had 44 interceptions, second only to Mel Renfro's 52. After leaving Dallas, Walls signed with the rival New York Giants and became a starter. He and his teammates beat the Buffalo Bills, 20–19, in Super Bowl XXV. Walls played a key role. In the closing minutes, the Bills were driving down the field in hopes of making a game-winning field goal. Running back Thurman Thomas broke free for 22 yards, and appeared headed for a much bigger gain. But Walls made a textbook open field tackle.

As a result, the Bills were forced to attempt a 47-yard field goal to win the game. Kicker Scott Norwood missed, and the Giants won.

Walls played for the Giants again in 1991, and part of 1992, before being traded to the Cleveland Browns. He retired after the 1993 season. He remains the only player to lead the NFL in interceptions three times.

"Everson had excellent hands," Brandt said. "He didn't drop interceptions."

33 Try out for Dallas Cowboys Cheerleaders

Here's a challenge: Try out for the Dallas Cowboys Cheerleaders.

The odds of making the elite squad aren't good. In fact, a young man probably has a better chance of making the Cowboys than a young woman has of making the cheerleaders.

Each spring, as many as 1,000 women from all over the country come to Dallas to audition for the cheerleaders. It's an annual event that's occurred for more than 35 years. During that time, the Dallas Cowboys Cheerleaders, in their skimpy blue-and-white uniforms, have become the most recognizable cheerleading squad in the NFL.

They put out best-selling calendars and posters, make television appearances, appear at corporate events, host cheerleading clinics, and travel overseas to perform for American troops. Most recently, the cheerleaders starred in a reality show on cable television.

Cowboys' general manager Tex Schramm dreamed up the Dallas Cowboys Cheerleaders in 1972. Schramm, a marketing genius, realized that pro football had become as much entertainment as sport. Sexy young women on the sidelines would boost the appeal even more. The cheerleaders were an immediate success. The original seven cheerleaders more closely resembled showgirls than traditional pom-pom girls.

"We wanted our cheerleaders to be pretty [and] sexy," Schramm said.

Women have never become a Dallas Cowboys Cheerleader for the money. Today, they're paid only $50 a game and aren't paid for their many hours of practice. But they are allowed to make money from personal appearances.

Candidates must be at least 18 years old and a high school graduate. They must successfully answer questions on the Cowboys, the NFL, cheerleaders' history, and current events. Women must be pretty (obviously), but there are no height or weight requirements.

"However, a lean figure is demanded by our uniform," guidelines say. "Cheerleaders gaining weight to an extreme are warned, then put on non-performing status, and finally terminated from the squad."

In 2007, 43 women made the squad. They ranged from 5' 1" to 5' 10" in height and weighed from 99 to 144 pounds. They were as young as 18 and as old as 33.

Cheerleaders must abide by a strict code of conduct. For instance, they can't date any player, coach, or employee of the Dallas Cowboys.

"The set of rules which govern each lady's appearance, performance, and moral character is lengthy and explicit," guidelines say. "Each girl is individually counseled on personal grooming, makeup, physical fitness, communications skills, media relations, and fan mail."

The cheerleaders' uniforms, consisting of short shorts and a low-cut blouse, are a carefully-guarded trademark. The Cowboys sue anyone who tries to copy them. When in uniform, "the Cheerleaders are not permitted to smoke, drink alcohol, or conduct themselves in any manner not becoming to the tradition of the Dallas Cowboys Cheerleaders."

One of their newest business ventures is a Dallas Cowboys Cheerleaders Barbie® doll. Introduced in 2007, the dolls are sold at Wal-Mart for about $35. They are dressed in authentic cheerleader uniforms. Other business ventures will surely follow.

The cheerleaders have morphed into a multi-million dollar business. But they remain "America's Sweethearts," their literature says. If you want to become a Dallas Cowboys Cheerleader, you'll need an appreciation for their rich tradition. As their website says,

"They are often imitated … They are never equaled … they are the Dallas Cowboys Cheerleaders!"

34 Super Bowl XXX—Third Win

The Cowboys desperately wanted to win three straight Super Bowls in the 1990s. They came extremely close. They won Super Bowl XXVII and XXVIII but lost in the NFC Championship Game the next year. In 1995, the Cowboys rebounded and won Super Bowl XXX.

The Triplets—Troy Aikman, Emmitt Smith, and Michael Irvin—formed the foundation of all three championships. Few teams have ever had such a dynamic trio of offensive players.

In Super Bowl XXX, Dallas jumped out to a 13–0 lead on two Chris Boniol field goals and a 3-yard touchdown reception by tight end Jay Novacek. The Cowboys seemed on their way to rolling over the Steelers, as they had the Bills in the two previous Super Bowls.

But the Steelers had no intention of lying down for the Cowboys. With 13 seconds remaining in the first half, quarterback Neil O'Donnell threw a 6-yard touchdown pass to pull the Steelers to within 13–7. The Steelers had a sudden boost of confidence heading into the locker room. The Cowboys, despite dominating the first half, held only a slim lead.

"We got comfortable when we got ahead 13–0 in the second quarter, and we didn't have the killer instinct," cornerback Larry Brown said.

The Steelers looked strong at the start of the second half. O'Donnell quickly moved the Steelers to midfield. But he then threw an errant pass that Brown intercepted and returned to the Pittsburgh 18-yard line. Two plays later, Emmitt Smith scored on a 1-yard run to extend Dallas' lead to 20–7.

Still, the Steelers didn't give up. At the start of the fourth quarter, they kicked a 46-yard field goal to make the score 20–10. Pittsburgh coach Bill Cowher then surprised the Cowboys with an onside kick attempt. The Steelers recovered the ball and seized more momentum. O'Donnell directed a 52-yard drive that ended with a 1-yard touchdown run by Bam Morris.

Pittsburgh, a 13-point underdog, had now pulled to within three points,

20–17. The Steelers held the Cowboys and got the ball back with 4:15 left in the game. O'Donnell had completed 14 of his last 15 passes and seemed unstoppable. But again, he threw a poor pass that Brown intercepted. He returned the ball 33 yards to the Pittsburgh 6-yard line. Two plays later, Smith scored his second touchdown on a 4-yard run. Dallas now had a comfortable 27–17 lead with 3:43 remaining. They stopped Pittsburgh from scoring again.

Brown, a 12th round draft pick in 1991, was named the game's Most Valuable Player for his two interceptions. He became the first cornerback ever to receive the Super Bowl MVP award. The honor provided a nice ending to a difficult year for Brown. In mid-November, his three-month-old son died after being born prematurely.

After the Super Bowl, Brown became a free agent. He signed a lucrative contract with the Oakland Raiders that included a $3.6 million bonus. But he never excelled as he had with the Cowboys. Brown had two injury-plagued seasons with Oakland before being cut. He then signed with Minnesota, but soon was released.

In 1998, the Cowboys re-signed Brown for extra depth in the secondary. He played sparingly and retired after the season. His career sputtered to an end after peaking in Super Bowl XXX. But he should be remembered fondly. His two interceptions allowed the Cowboys to beat Pittsburgh in the Super Bowl and make history.

No previous team had ever won three Super Bowls in four years.

35 The 2007 Cowboys—Disappointment

The Cowboys began the 2007 season with loads of uncertainty. They had a new coach, a promising but still unproven quarterback, and a shaky defense. Fortunately, none of the three turned out to be a problem.

The Cowboys rolled to a 13–3 record, equaling the best record in franchise history. Coach Wade Phillips won over players with his laidback approach, a sharp contrast from his dictatorial predecessor, Bill Parcells. Quarterback Tony Romo, who had a magical second half in 2006, proved his performance was no fluke. In 2007, he threw 36 touchdown passes, setting a team record. Owner Jerry Jones rewarded him with a six-year, $67 million contract. The defense, stocked with young players, coalesced into a rock-solid unit. Third-year linebacker DeMarcus Ware had 14 sacks and was named to the Pro Bowl.

In all, 12 players received Pro Bowl honors, a league high.

The Cowboys' offense proved to be their greatest strength. The unit scored 455 points, second-most in team history. Marion Barber rushed for 975 yards and scored 10 touchdowns, even though he didn't start a game. Receiver Terrell Owens rebounded from a mediocre 2006 and had one of his finest seasons. He caught 81 passes for 1,355 yards and scored 15 touchdowns.

Fifth-year tight end Jason Witten had an even better season. He caught 96 passes for 1,145 yards and scored seven touchdowns. Witten, 6' 5" and 266 pounds, has an unstoppable combination of size, speed, and route-running ability.

Rookie kicker Nick Folk, a sixth-round draft pick from Arizona, turned out to be the team's brightest surprise. He made 26 of 31 field goals, including a 53-yarder. He was perfect from 40 to 49 yards.

After the Cowboys finished 13–3 record and received a first-round playoff bye, most people expected them to march to the Super Bowl. However, the pesky New York Giants, whom the Cowboys had beaten twice, got in the way. They pulled off a monumental upset, beating the Cowboys at home, 21–17, in their first postseason game. Dallas looked lethargic and committed a rash of costly penalties. They played like a team that was either overconfident or rusty from the bye week.

Mistakes abounded everywhere. Backup tight end Anthony Fasano dropped a touchdown pass. Romo missed a wide-open Owens for what could have been another touchdown. Receiver Patrick Crayton inexplicably quit running on a deep pattern, allowing Romo's throw to sail over his head, another potential touchdown squandered. The Cowboys also killed themselves with penalties, committing of 11 for 84 yards. Over and over, penalties ended drives or put the Cowboys in deep holes.

The Giants, to their credit, played well. In the first half, they managed to put little pressure on Romo. But in the second half, they made adjustments and kept Romo on the run. He had to leave the pocket and make hurried throws. Romo, after a spectacular regular season, played like an unproven backup.

Despite a mediocre performance, he still had a chance to pull out a win late in the game. But on the final play, he threw an interception in the end zone to finish off the Cowboys' season.

"I'm dying," Jones said afterward.

So were fans. The 2007 Cowboys teased them with an extraordinary regular season, only to lay an egg in the playoffs. People had already scripted the ending to the season. The Cowboys would dust off their first-round playoff opponent, beat the Green Bay Packers at home in the NFC Championship, and then topple the previously unbeaten New England Patriots in Super Bowl XLII.

But the Giants, a 10–6 team, took the fairytale and ripped it in two. The season's positives immediately slipped from memory, replaced by an aching sense of what could have been.

36 Troy Aikman—Later Years

Troy Aikman's career included Super Bowl championships and last-place finishes. When he was a rookie starter in 1989, the Cowboys finished a dismal 1–15. Four years later, they won the first of three Super Bowls in the 1990s.

By the end of Aikman's 12-year career, however, the Cowboys had returned to mediocrity. In his last year in 2000, Aikman had a miserable year and the Cowboys finished 5–11, missing the playoffs. He threw twice as many interceptions as touchdowns. His quarterback rating of 64.3 was his worst since his rookie year and the lowest among the league's starting quarterbacks. In one game, Aikman threw five interceptions.

His retirement was hastened by an injury. Late in the 2000 season, in a game against Washington, Aikman rolled out to pass. As he looked for an open receiver, linebacker LaVar Arrington made a hard but clean hit on Aikman, knocking him out of bounds. Aikman's head bounced off the turf, and he suffered the 10th concussion of his career. He would never play again, worried about the cumulative effect of the head injuries.

After the Cowboys won Super Bowl XXX following the 1995 season, Aikman and the team declined. From 1996 to 2000, the Cowboys compiled a record of only 39–41. They made the playoffs twice, but never advanced. Aikman, who prospered under coach Jimmy Johnson early in his career, had three coaches in his final five seasons. He didn't agree with some of their offensive philosophies, but went along and tried to adapt.

Aikman had a weaker supporting cast as well. Many top players from the Super Bowl teams signed lucrative free agent contracts with other clubs. In addition, the Cowboys made poor draft selections, limiting the influx of new talent.

In his early years, Aikman had taken a tremendous beating behind a weak offensive line. He began paying the price. Aikman suffered chronic back pain and missed five games in 1998, two in 1999 and five in 2000.

His retirement, however, wasn't entirely voluntary. The Cowboys would have had to pay Aikman a $7 million bonus to bring him back in 2001, and owner Jerry Jones didn't think he was worth the price. Aikman, at only 34 years of age, was finished.

"My time has come," he said at an emotional press conference.

Five years later, in his first year of eligibility, Aikman was elected to the Pro Football Hall of Fame. His induction came as no surprise. Besides leading the Cowboys to three Super Bowl wins, Aikman won more games in a single decade, 90, than any quarterback in NFL history. He played in six straight Pro Bowls from 1992 to 1997 and set dozens of Cowboys passing records. Some may never be broken.

His teammates appreciated Aikman's contributions and hated to see him retire.

"His leadership and focus are what made us the team we were in the 1990s," Emmitt Smith said.

37 Searching for a Quarterback

After Troy Aikman retired in 2000, the Cowboys didn't have a proven backup waiting in the wings. During the 2001 season, coaches experimented with four different quarterbacks started. None did well enough to seize the job.

Rookie Quincy Carter started eight games. Ryan Leaf, a former first-round flop with San Diego, got three starts. Anthony Wright, a free agent, started three games. Clint Stoerner, another free agent, started twice.

All proved to be expendable, and Dallas finished 5–11. Carter got the longest look simply because the Cowboys had invested the most in him: a second-round pick. Owner Jerry Jones was Carter's biggest advocate. He pushed for the team to draft Carter early, when many pro scouts thought he was a mid-round selection at best.

Jones, no doubt, would like a do-over with the pick. Carter had an erratic arm. He became flustered in the pocket and scrambled too often. He made poor decisions and displayed weak leadership skills.

The Cowboys hoped Carter would improve in his second year. He did, slightly, but he still showed no signs of being the quarterback of the future. After the Cowboys lost three of their first five games in 2002, coaches turned to an unproven but intriguing prospect: Chad Hutchinson. Hutchinson was a 25-year-old rookie who had spent four years as a professional baseball player. He briefly reached the major leagues with the St. Louis Cardinals, but then returned to the minors. That's when he decided to try pro football.

The Cowboys signed Hutchinson to a seven-year contract that included a $3.1 million signing bonus. Hutchinson looked the part of a franchise quarterback. He stood 6' 5" and had an Aikman-like arm. As a two-year starter at Stanford University, Hutchinson completed 60 percent of his passes and threw 20 touchdowns.

The Cowboys waited patiently as Hutchinson got re-acclimated to football. He made some brilliant throws and some awful ones. Unlike Carter,

Hutchinson wasn't mobile. He stood in the pocket too long and took unnecessary sacks. He didn't learn to throw the ball away when he had no open receivers. After another 5–11 finish in 2002, the Cowboys gave up on Hutchinson. He's now out of football.

In 2003, Bill Parcells took over as Cowboys' coach. He named Carter the starter, primarily because he didn't have a better choice. Carter finally displayed some encouraging signs. He completed 58 percent of his passes and threw 17 touchdowns, although he also threw 21 interceptions.

Still, the Cowboys finished 10–6, their first winning season in five years. They made the playoffs as a wild-card team, but lost in the first round. Despite Carter's improved performance in 2003, Parcells still lacked confidence in him. Just before the 2004 season, the Cowboys released Carter. There were rumors of a failed drug test, but the team never confirmed the reports.

Even if the rumors were false, Carter's lackluster performance—especially for a top draft pick—justified his release. Without Carter, the Cowboys turned to 41-year-old Vinny Testaverde in 2004. The Tampa Bay Buccaneers had taken Testaverde with their first pick in 1987, and he had enjoyed a productive career with four teams.

Parcells liked veteran quarterbacks and trusted Testaverde not to lose games with dumb mistakes. Testaverde had a decent season, completing 60 percent of his passes and throwing 17 touchdowns. But the Cowboys took a step backward with a 6–10 record.

The quarterback merry-go-round continued in 2005 with the arrival of another veteran quarterback, Drew Bledsoe. Bledsoe was the No. 1 pick of the New England Patriots in 1993, and had a solid career before losing his starting job to Tom Brady. Bledsoe then spent three years with the Buffalo Bills before coming to Dallas.

Bledsoe provided stability, starting all 16 games. The Cowboys finished 9–7, but missed the playoffs. In 2006, Bledsoe returned as starter and struggled. At halftime of the sixth game, Parcells turned to Bledsoe's backup, Tony Romo.

Romo, a fourth-year free agent, surprised fans and coaches with his accurate passing and big-play ability. He started the remaining 10 games of the season, and completed 65 percent of his passes with 19 touchdowns. The Cowboys compiled a 9–7 record and earned a wild-card playoff spot. They lost in the opening round, 21–20 to Seattle, after Romo mishandled the snap on a potential game-winning field goal.

Despite his blunder and the team's early playoff exit, Romo provided some optimism for the future. Time would tell whether he'd be the next Troy Aikman or just another bust.

38 Tony Romo

At last, the Cowboys have another franchise quarterback, the first since Troy Aikman retired in 2000. In his first full year as a starter in 2007, Romo built on his outstanding play of the previous season. He completed 64 percent of his passes, threw a club-record 36 touchdowns, and led the team to a 13–3 finish. He also was named to the Pro Bowl for the second straight year.

He made a believer out of owner Jerry Jones, who signed Romo to a six-year, $67 million contract. A few years earlier, no one could have imagined that Romo would emerge as a superstar. He came to Dallas in 2003 as a free agent out of Eastern Illinois. Quickly, he became buried on the depth chart.

He watched the quarterbacks in front of him and learned. Slowly, he began to gain the coaches' confidence. He didn't have a rifle arm, and he wasn't huge or particularly fast. However, Romo knew how to make plays and he outlasted several other backups to earn the No. 2 spot behind Drew Bledsoe in 2006.

In the sixth game of the season, with Bledsoe struggling, coach Bill Parcells gave Romo the reins. He played the second half against the New York Giants, and completed 14 of 25 passes. He threw two touchdowns, but his three interceptions helped the Giants win, 36–22.

Still, Parcells stuck with Romo. It was a good decision. Romo led the Cowboys to six wins in their final 10 games. He completed 65 percent of

Tony Romo (9), pictured third from left along with Chad Hutchinson (7), Quincy Carter (17), and Clint Stoerner (5), was just another candidate hoping to fills the shoes of Troy Aikman when this photo was taken at Cowboys' training camp in San Antonio in July 2003.

his passes and threw 19 touchdowns, versus only 13 interceptions. He played with a childlike enthusiasm that spread to his teammates and fans.

The Cowboys finished 9–7, good enough to squeak into the playoffs as a wild-card team. Fans and players now believed in him. Considering Romo's fairytale season, people thought he might take the Cowboys all the way to the Super Bowl.

He didn't. In the first playoff game, Dallas faced the Seattle Seahawks. The Cowboys played well against the more experienced team but trailed, 21–20, late in the game. Romo then put the Cowboys in a position to win. He drove them to the Seattle 2-yard line with only 1:19 remaining. If the Cowboys could make an easy 19-yard field goal, they would win their first playoff game in 11 years. Romo doubled as the field goal holder. He hadn't bobbled a snap all year, but this time he did. A perfect snap slid through his hands.

With defenders approaching, Romo grabbed the ball off the turf and began running around the left end. For a split-second, it looked like he might score a touchdown to win the game. Wouldn't that have been an ending?

Instead, Romo was caught from behind and tackled on the 2-yard line. The season suddenly ended. Romo took the loss hard, crying in the locker room and apologizing to fans in a post-game press conference. In the off season, however, Romo managed to shake off the monumental mistake and regroup for 2007.

He turned in one of the best seasons ever for a Dallas quarterback. He made headlines with his play on the field and off the field. He began dating Hollywood star Jessica Simpson, enhancing his unlikely rags-to-riches story.

Life is good for Tony Romo.

39 Searching for a Coach

Jimmy Johnson had a remarkable run as Cowboys' coach. In only five seasons, he transformed the Cowboys from a 1–15 team to a two-team Super Bowl winner. But then owner Jerry Jones fired Johnson, their massive egos unable to co-exist any longer.

Jones then hired and fired three coaches over the next 10 years: Barry Switzer, Chan Gailey, and Dave Campo. None came close to producing the results of Johnson. The first of Jones' hires after Johnson seemed the most unlikely. Former Oklahoma coach Barry Switzer had never coached in the NFL. And he hadn't coached, period, in five years since leaving OU.

Cowboy fans initially had a hard time accepting Switzer because of his

Oklahoma ties. But they welcomed him once they believed he could produce another Super Bowl title. When Switzer joined the Cowboys in 1994, they still were the most talented team in the league. Despite his lack of NFL coaching experience, Switzer could hardly fail with the players he had been handed.

For two years, he succeeded. In 1994, the Cowboys finished 12–4 and met the San Francisco 49ers in the NFC title game. They lost, 38–28. In 1995, the Cowboys again finished 12–4. This time, they swept through the playoffs and hammered the Pittsburgh Steelers, 27–17, in Super Bowl XXX.

The Switzer experiment seemed to be working. But Switzer, unlike Johnson, couldn't keep the Cowboys on top. In 1996, they fell to 10–6 and lost in the second round of the playoffs. The Cowboys' slide accelerated in 1997, Switzer's fourth year. They dropped to 6–10, the team's first losing season since 1990. At the end of the season, Jones fired Switzer.

To replace Switzer, Jones made another surprising hire: Chan Gailey, offensive coordinator of the Pittsburgh Steelers. Gailey may have been widely known around the NFL, but few Cowboy fans had heard of him. Plus, he'd never been a head coach at any level.

Gailey, however, led the Cowboys to a 10–6 record in 1998—a major turnaround from the 6–10 mark the previous year. Fans and players, once wary of Gailey, began to embrace him. Maybe Gailey would have a long, successful tenure, or maybe not.

In Gailey's second season, the Cowboys dropped to 8–8. Quarterback Troy Aikman became disenchanted with Gailey's offensive schemes. The Cowboys couldn't score enough points to be competitive. They lost by scores of 13–6, 13–9, and 13–10. Without Aikman's support, Gailey didn't have a chance of staying. Jones fired him after the 1999 season.

Next, Jones picked Cowboys' defensive coordinator Dave Campo to be head coach. Players liked Campo. He was a nice guy, but few viewed him as head coaching material. With his mellow personality, Campo didn't inspire players or excite fans.

From the beginning, he seemed in over his head. The Cowboys lost three of their first four games under Campo and wound up 5–11. The losses included two shutouts, 31–0 to the Tennessee Titans and 27–0 to the Indianapolis Colts. In 2001, and again in 2002, the Cowboys finished an identical 5–11. That wasn't the kind of consistency Jones wanted. He fired Campo after the 2002 season. The Cowboys seemed to be in shambles.

Where would Jones turn next? Another college coach, an NFL assistant? Few could have guessed the man Jones would hire.

40 Landing Parcells

Jerry Jones surprised fans, players, and the entire NFL by hiring Bill Parcells as coach in 2003. No one could have imagined that Parcells, who had won two Super Bowls, would want to work for the meddlesome, egotistical Jones.

But Parcells said he wanted to coach a winner, and he thought the Cowboys had the potential to get back on top. If nothing else, Parcells's arrival sparked renewed interest in the Cowboys. After three straight 5–11 seasons under Dave Campo, they had faded from view.

Jones couldn't have hired a more prominent, successful coach. During his 15-year NFL coaching career, Parcells had won two Super Bowls with the New York Giants and guided the New England Patriots to a Super Bowl that they didn't win. Parcells was viewed as a modern-day Vince Lombardi: tough, surly, even mean. But he was a winner—and that's all Jones cared about. Because of the Cowboys' decline, Jones was willing to share the limelight with a coach he thought could restore the team's luster.

Parcells, for his part, viewed the Cowboys job as a chance to redeem himself. His last stop had been with New York Jets, and he failed to take them to the Super Bowl. He knew Jones had deep pockets and a commitment to winning. Parcells figured he could endure Jones looking over his shoulder if it meant a chance to win a third Super Bowl.

The media predicted a rocky marriage between Jones and Parcells. If Jones and Jimmy Johnson couldn't co-exist, how would Jones and Parcells?

The 2003 season arrived with great buzz. Fans hoped Parcells could work his magic on the Cowboys the way he had with the Giants and Patriots.

The season, however, started out badly. The Cowboys lost their opener, 27–13, to the Atlanta Falcons at home. The next game, the Cowboys beat the Giants, 35–32, in a thrilling overtime contest. The Cowboys then won four straight games to stand at 5–1. Fans loved Parcells, nicknamed Tuna.

In the final 10 games, the Cowboys returned to mediocrity. They won five and lost five. They suffered two shutouts, 16–0 to Tampa Bay and 12–0 to New England. But the Cowboys still finished 10–6 overall, their best record since 1998.

More importantly, they were back in the playoffs. Fans envisioned Parcells taking the Cowboys back to the Super Bowl, but the script proved unrealistic. The Cowboys fell to the Carolina Panthers, 29–10, in a wild-card game. Still, no one complained much. Parcells had made a big splash in his first year, and seemed to have the Cowboys headed in the right direction.

However, the team did a belly flop in 2004, finishing 6–10. In the opener, Minnesota hammered the Cowboys, 35–17. Dallas rebounded with two straight wins, then lost three in a row. The Cowboys were hurt by not having a top-notch quarterback. Parcells started 41-year-old Vinny Testaverde. He took over for Quincy Carter, a former starter whom Parcells released before the season began.

In 2005, Parcell's third year, he brought in another veteran quarterback, Drew Bledsoe. Bledsoe had played under Parcells at New England and had some fine years. At 33, he was a child compared to Testaverde and a definite upgrade. He led the Cowboys to a 9–7 finish, but it wasn't good enough to make the playoffs.

After three seasons, Parcells had compiled a disappointing 25–23 record with no playoff wins. He still had two years remaining on his contract, enough time to revive the Cowboys. In 2006, the Cowboys finished 9–7 again and earned a wild-card playoff spot. Again, they couldn't advance. The Cowboys lost, 21–20, to the Seattle Seahawks in the first round.

People began to wonder if Parcells would return for a fifth season. Jones said he wanted Parcells back. But Parcells decided he didn't want the job any longer. Without giving a specific reason, Parcells resigned. He announced his move in a brief prepared statement released by the club and didn't face the media to take questions.

Parcells turned out to be an enigma. He arrived with a splash, didn't meet expectations, then slipped out the back door.

41 Wade Phillips

Few people expected the Cowboys to hire Wade Phillips as their head coach in 2007. He and Norv Turner, a former Cowboys assistant, emerged as finalists for the job. Turner, who was offensive coordinator during the Super Bowl days of the early 1990s, seemed to be the odds-on favorite. Instead, owner Jerry Jones turned to Phillips, a 60-year-old defensive specialist who had been moderately successfully as head coach in Buffalo and Denver.

When the Cowboys got off to a roaring start in 2007, Phillips seemed like the perfect hire. He had a calm temperament, unlike his predecessor, the fiery Bill Parcells. The Cowboys, a young team, seemed to respond well to the grandfatherly Phillips.

In the opener, Dallas outscored the New York Giants, 45–35. They won their next three games by wide margins, scoring an average of 35 points a game. A slim 25–24 win over Buffalo gave the Cowboys a 5–0 start. You couldn't ask for better beginning by a first-year coach.

In the sixth game, the Cowboys faced their toughest challenge of the year: the undefeated New England Patriots. The Pats beat the Cowboys at Texas Stadium, 48–27, but few faulted Phillips for the loss. No team would beat New England all year. After the loss, the Cowboys reeled off seven straight wins to reach 12–1, a franchise first. Phillips seemed to have a steady hand on the controls. Fans didn't seem concerned when the Cowboys dropped two of their last three games to finish at 13–3.

In hindsight, people probably should have sounded the alarm. Dallas couldn't manage a touchdown in losing 10–6 to the Philadelphia Eagles or 27–6 to the Washington Redskins. In the first half of the season, the Cowboys averaged 33 points per game. In the last half, they averaged only 23 points. After losing badly to Washington, the Cowboys limped into the playoffs.

Because of their glittering record, they earned a bye week. Coaches and players usually say they love the extra time to prepare for the first playoff game. It gives players a chance to recover mentally and physically from the grind of the regular season.

On the other hand, a bye week can disrupt a team's timing and halt its momentum. In the Cowboys' case, the week off hurt. Dallas came out flat against the underdog New York Giants. Receivers dropped critical passes. Quarterback Tony Romo missed wide-open receivers. Players on both sides of the ball committed dumb and costly penalties.

The result: a shocking 21–17 loss to the Giants.

How much blame should Phillips receive? Tough question. In hindsight, Phillips probably let the Cowboys get overconfident down the stretch. He probably minimized the two losses late in the season. During the bye week, Phillips probably loosened the reins a bit too much on players.

For instance, he didn't object to star players leaving town on vacation during the week off. Romo took a much-publicized trip to Mexico with his glamorous girlfriend, Jessica Simpson.

Still, pro athletes are adults and should be allowed to have a personal life. But maybe, just maybe, the Cowboys would have been sharper against the Giants if Phillips had cracked the whip during the bye week. He could have insisted that players stay in town. He could have called daily practices. Most of all, he could have instilled a sense of urgency in the players. He could have emphasized that a 13–3 record means nothing in the playoffs.

After the loss, all eyes focused on Jones. Would he criticize Phillips? Would he even fire him? The loss to the Giants gave Phillips an 0–4 playoff record as a head coach. Did Jones think Phillips couldn't produce a champion?

Jones, instead, gave Phillips a vote of confidence—not a ringing endorsement, but a guarantee that Phillips would return in 2008.

"It's not an issue," Jones said. "He's our head coach."

However, with Jerry Jones as boss, a coach can never feel totally secure. After all, Jimmy Johnson won back-to-back Super Bowls, and Jones fired him. Phillips should be given credit for the Cowboys' 13–3 record, tied for the best in club history. He could have the same success in 2008, and the players could learn from the first-round playoff exit. The Cowboys could go all the way to a Super Bowl title, and Phillips could be named Coach of the Year. Or, they could fall short again, and Jones could send Phillips packing.

Stay tuned. With Jones as owner, anything is possible.

42 Daryl Johnston

Daryl Johnston never rushed for more than 212 yards in a single season. He never scored more than three rushing touchdowns in a season. His totals for his 11-year career seem almost embarrassing: 753 yards rushing with a 3.2-yards-per-carry average.

But statistics aren't kept on the number of hole-opening blocks a fullback makes. In Johnston's case, he cleared the way for running back Emmitt Smith hundreds and hundreds of times. Without the 6' 2", 238-pound Johnston as his lead blocker, Smith might never have become the NFL's all-time rushing leader. All eyes, naturally, focused on Smith as he darted through defenses and piled up more than 17,000 yards as a Cowboy.

Meanwhile, Johnston remained back at the line of scrimmage doing the dirty work: moving out defensive linemen and linebackers. Smith never took Johnston for granted. In his book, *The Emmitt Zone*, Smith praises Johnston, nicknamed the Moose.

"Nobody's tougher than Moose, nobody works any harder, and no one appreciates him more than I do," Smith wrote. "Week after week, he sticks his head in the tightest holes and blasts them open. I really don't know where I'd be without the guy. Moose allows me to be the pro runner I'd always hoped to be."

Daryl Johnston scores a touchdown in the NFL Divisional Playoff game against the Carolina Panthers on January 5, 1997.

Johnston never complained about his lack of attention. In fact, he seemed to enjoy the anonymity. He cheered Emmitt on as much as anyone, instead of grousing about not getting more carries. Johnston understood and embraced his role on a championship team.

"One of the things I really enjoyed during my playing career was hearing the fans cheer for me, hearing them call 'Mooooose!' every time I touched the ball," he wrote in his book, *Watching Football: Discovering the Game Within the Game.* "It showed that they looked beyond the statistics to appreciate a guy for the behind-the-scenes work that he was doing, for being part of a team and doing whatever it takes to win."

Indeed, Johnston was just as important to the Cowboys' three Super Bowl titles as Smith, Troy Aikman, or Michael Irvin. Johnston kept Aikman from getting sacked just as he kept Smith from getting tackled at the line of scrimmage. Occasionally, when defenses expected a pass to Irvin, Aikman would hand the ball off to the burly fullback and he'd rumble for a first down.

Johnston was never a breakaway threat. Speed and shifty moves weren't his game. But No. 48 provided a steady, comforting presence to fans and teammates alike from 1989 to 1999. In his first eight years, Johnston didn't miss a single game because of injury.

Johnston rarely scared opponents with his rushing, but was an effective receiving threat. In 1993, the season the Cowboys won Super Bowl XXVIII, Johnston caught 50 passes for 372 yards. He had seasons with 44 and 43 catches. For his career, Johnston had 14 receiving touchdowns, compared with only eight on the ground.

He retired in 1999 because of neck problems. He injured his neck in 1997 and had to have two vertebrae fused. He continued for two more seasons before leaving the game.

"Late in my career, I'd watch myself on tape, and I could see I wasn't playing the same," Johnston wrote. "I had been hurt at various times earlier in my career, but those were pain-related issues, which I could deal with. But the neck injury was different."

After retiring, Johnston became a color analyst for Fox television. His comments are insightful, as you would expect from a high school valedictorian and graduate of Syracuse University.

"I've been criticized in some circles for not being tough enough on the air," he said. "But I've been there, and I know that everyone who has ever played the game has been knocked on his behind now and then. So, unless a player has done something wrong or unethical, I don't get on him."

Spoken like a true gentleman.

43 Jay Novacek

Jay Novacek was a tight end who played like a wide receiver. Normally, tight ends are known for their blocking. But Novacek became a reliable receiving threat during the Cowboys' championship years of the early 1990s. At 6' 4" and 234 pounds, Novacek was easy for Troy Aikman to spot. He had the speed and elusiveness to consistently get in the open.

In 1990, Novacek joined the Cowboys as a free agent after five years with the St. Louis/Phoenix Cardinals. He had had a solid but unspectacular career. The Cowboys thought they were getting a nice role player. Instead, Novacek developed into the best tight end in the NFL. In his first year with the Cowboys, Novacek caught 59 passes for 657 yards and scored four touchdowns. In 1991, he put up almost identical numbers: 59 catches for 664 yards and four touchdowns. Starting in 1991, Novacek made five straight Pro Bowl appearances and became the Cowboys' all-time leading receiver for a tight end.

He had his best year in 1992 when he caught 68 passes and scored six touchdowns. That was the year the Cowboys demolished the Buffalo Bills, 52–17, in Super Bowl XXVII. Novacek played a key role in the win. He scored the Cowboys' first touchdown and led all Dallas receivers with seven catches.

Coach Jimmy Johnson recalled the TD pass to Novacek.

"We caught them in two-deep coverage and Novacek split the middle of the field, between the safeties, on a 23-yard catch and run for a touchdown," Johnson said. "The game was tied and beginning to unfold inevitably in our direction."

In Super Bowl XXVIII, a rematch with the Bills, Novacek had another big game. He caught five passes in the Cowboys' 30–13 win. Novacek was "sure-handed" and "deceptively quick," running back Emmitt Smith said.

"Jay always finds a way to get open," Smith wrote in *The Emmitt Zone*. "With that unorthodox running style of his, he lulls people to sleep, then

Jay Novacek catches a pass during pregame warm ups before the NFC Championship Game against the Green Bay Packers on January 14, 1996.

beats them badly. We call Jay 'Paycheck' because he's so clutch."

Novacek retired after the 1995 season and the Cowboys' 27–17 victory over the Pittsburgh Steelers in Super Bowl XXX. Chronic back problems hastened his decision.

Before coming to the NFL, Novacek had an outstanding college career at Wyoming. He was an All-American tight end in 1984, and set an NCAA record for yards-per-catch for the position. He also was a star track athlete, earning All-American honors in the decathlon.

Even though he's retired, Novacek is still a cowboy—in the true sense of the word. He runs a 3,500–acre ranch in Nebraska where people hunt, stay in a lodge, and eat home-cooked meals. It's called the Upper 84 Ranch, a nod to his jersey number with the Cowboys.

"The most satisfying thing about the ranch is that I'm doing all the things I love to do—from the horses, to the cattle, to hunting, to putting on cattle drives for clients," Novacek said. "When I want to unwind and relax, it's on the ranch."

44 Jason Witten

The Cowboys have had a succession of great tight ends, but Jason Witten has become the best of all. In only five seasons, he's broken the team record for receptions and yardage for a tight end. Witten, who is 6' 5" and 266 pounds, is a devastating blocker as well as an outstanding receiver. He runs tremendous routes, consistently finding openings in the secondary, and he rarely drops passes.

Witten has become quarterback Tony Romo's favorite target. In 2007, Witten caught 96 passes, only six shy of the NFL record for tight ends. Witten had even more receptions than the Cowboys' most famous receiver, Terrell Owens, who caught 81 passes.

The Cowboys drafted Witten in the third round of the 2003 draft. He began his college career at Tennessee as a defensive end before switching to offense. He quickly became a standout. Witten set a school record for receptions and receiving yards in a single season by a tight end.

As a rookie with the Cowboys, Witten made an immediate impact. He started seven games and caught 35 passes. In his second year, 2004, Witten became a star. He had 87 receptions for almost 1,000 yards and scored six touchdowns. He made the Pro Bowl and has returned every year since.

In 2007, Witten made a play that will be talked about for years to come. In a game against the Philadelphia Eagles midway through the season, Witten caught a 23-yard pass across the middle. He took a huge hit, and his helmet popped off. Witten didn't hesitate to look for it. He didn't fall to the ground to avoid taking a blow to the head. Witten kept on running with the ball toward the end zone, hair flapping in the wind, and he picked up another 30 yards.

Witten is one tough guy. But after the game, he downplayed the catch and run.

"I'm a tight end," he said. "I can't go down right away."

His best performance in 2007 occurred in the 13th game, against the Detroit Lions. Witten had 15 catches, setting a team record for receptions in a single game. He broke a 40-year-old record of 13 set by Lance Rentzel. Witten has surpassed the receiving records set by Jay Novacek, the most prolific tight end in Cowboys' history and a five-time Pro Bowl selection. During his Dallas career from 1990 to 1995, Novacek caught 339 passes for 3,576 yards. Witten now has 348 catches for 3,983 yards.

Before Novacek, the Cowboys had two other great tight ends. Doug Cosbie played from 1979 to 1988 and made the Pro Bowl three times. Before him, Billy Joe DuPree starred from 1973 to 1983. He also was a three-time Pro Bowl selection.

Novacek, Cosbie, and DuPree praise Witten. DuPree, who still lives in Dallas, visited a Cowboys' practice in late 2007 to watch Witten.

"Jason has a combination of Doug Cosbie, Billy Joe DuPree, and Jay Novacek," DuPree said. "He has quick feet, and most people probably don't understand that. He's a little faster, a little quicker, than they anticipate."

After the 2006 season, owner Jerry Jones rewarded Witten with a six-year,

$28 million contract extension. The contract acknowledged that Witten has become one of the league's top tight ends and also a team leader.

Coaches love Witten because he is an outstanding player and a solid person. He does a wide range of charity work, and has formed the Jason Witten S.C.O.R.E. Foundation to help families affected by domestic violence. In 2007, he was a finalist for the NFL Man of the Year Award for his community involvement.

Look for Witten to keep receiving awards for his on-the-field and off-the-field activity for years to come.

45 Deion Sanders

Neon Deion—that's his nickname, and it fits to a tee. Deion Sanders was flashy, whether it comes to his wardrobe or his style of play. Now that he's retired, Sanders expresses his individuality with sometimes outrageous clothes. He definitely brightens the telecast when he's doing color commentary for NFL games.

As a player, Sanders had a flashy, one-of-a-kind style. He was such a talented cornerback that many teams didn't even throw his way. That's the ultimate compliment for a defensive back. Some say Sanders is the greatest cornerback to ever play in the NFL. "Prime Time," another of his nicknames, had a remarkable combination of speed, quickness, timing, and football savvy. When he scored a touchdown, Sanders even had a celebration dance all his own.

Sanders never tried to be humble. He knew he was the best and he acted like it. He had the skills to justify his bravado. "I was never good," Sanders said. "I was always great."

Sanders joined the Cowboys in 1995 as a free agent. Owner Jerry Jones lured him away from the rival San Francisco 49ers, where in his only season there he scored three touchdowns and was named Defensive Player

Deion Sanders, shown here during a September 1997 game, had a way of lifting fans out of their seats with his spectacular athletic ability and playmaking.

of the Year. Sanders represented the biggest free agent signing in Dallas Cowboy history, and one of the biggest ever. Jones gave Sanders a $35 million contract that included a $12.9 million signing bonus. No one else could have demanded that much money. But Jones desperately wanted to win another Super Bowl, and he knew Sanders could be the key.

The year before, the 49ers had beaten the Cowboys in the NFC Championship Game. The loss ended the Cowboys' bid for an unprecedented third-straight Super Bowl win. Jones wanted to get back on top, so he began courting Sanders after the 1994 season ended. Sanders knew he could be the difference maker for the Cowboys, and that appealed to him. In addition, Jones offered him the chance to play offense. Sanders' breakaway speed made him a receiving threat.

Despite the hype surrounding Sanders, teammates and coaches welcomed him.

"When a guy like Deion is on the other team, and he goes through his antics and showboating, you tend not to like him," said Joe Avezzano, former Cowboys' special teams coach. "When he gets on your team and you see that it's just part of his personality and you get to know the person—not just the player—then you find out what a good person and teammate he is."

In his first year with Dallas in 1995, Sanders missed the first four games with an injury, but then solidified the defense and helped the Cowboys roll to a 12–4 record. In the opening round of the playoffs, Sanders scored his first touchdown as a Cowboy on a reverse play. Then in Super Bowl XXX, Sanders caught a 47-yard pass to set up a touchdown that gave Dallas a 10–0 lead. The Cowboys went on to defeat the Pittsburgh Steelers, 27–17.

Sanders had his finest performance as a Cowboy in 1998. In a Monday night game against the New York Giants, Sanders scored one touchdown on an interception return and another on a punt return. He also caught a 55-yard pass as the Cowboys hammered the New York Giants, 31–7.

"That was an unbelievable performance," Avezzano said.

Sanders finished the 1998 season with five interceptions and led the league with a 15.6-yard average on punt returns. After the 1999 season, Sanders left the Cowboys for a big free-agent contract with the Washington Redskins. He played one year and retired. Then, four years later, Sanders came back to play two seasons with the Baltimore Ravens. He then retired for good to the broadcast booth.

As a color analyst, Sanders gets to remain in the spotlight. He wouldn't have it any other way.

46 Terrell Owens

Terrell Owens a Dallas Cowboy? The idea would have seemed absurd a few years ago. After all, Owens mocked the Cowboys as a San Francisco 49er in 2000. He caught a touchdown pass and then ran to the star at the center of the field and raised his arms in celebration. When he scored a second touchdown, Owens headed for the star again. But Dallas safety George Teague, to his credit, tackled Owens before he could get there.

By 2006, the Cowboys had gone 10 years without a playoff victory. Owner Jerry Jones wanted to win so badly that he put the Owens incident behind him and offered the flashy wide receiver a three-year, $25 million contract. The deal was amazing because his previous team, the Philadelphia Eagles, had released Owens midway through the 2005 season over his disruptive conduct. His insistence on a new contract and his criticism of quarterback Donovan McNabb finally became too much for Eagles' coach Andy Reid.

Many people thought Owens would be a divisive force with the Cowboys, as he had been with the Eagles. Owens, however, surprised people. He worked hard during training camp, didn't make any disruptive comments and acted like the ultimate team player.

Owens may have impressed people with his attitude, but he didn't impress anyone with his performance. He dropped so many passes that people kept a running total. The number quickly climbed into the double digits. Quarterback Drew Bledsoe, who started the first six games of 2006, preferred throwing to the other receiver, sure-handed Terry Glenn.

When Tony Romo became the starter in the seventh game, Owens's production picked up. He ended up having a good season, catching 85 passes for 1,180 yards and scoring a league-high 13 receiving touchdowns. But Jones still expected more from his $25 million player. Jones expected

Greeted by unprecedented hype when he came to the Cowboys in 2006, Terrell Owens has managed to become a solid playmaker for the Cowboys.

Owens to be a superstar and to elevate the entire team with his play.

Heading into the 2007 season, fans had relatively low expectations of Owens. Immediately, however, he began performing like a Pro Bowl player again. In the opening 45–35 win over the New York Giants, Owens scored two touchdowns. In the third game, he caught eight passes and solidified his role as Romo's go-to guy. Owens saved his biggest performance for the tenth game, catching eight passes and scoring four touchdowns in an important 28–23 win over the Washington Redskins.

Owens ended 2007 with 81 catches for 1,355 yards. He scored a team-record 15 receiving touchdowns. As much as anyone, Owens accounted for the Cowboys' superlative 13–3 record. He made the Pro Bowl for the first time since 2004. He and his teammates, however, played miserably in their first and only playoff game. They suffered a shocking 21–17 loss to the wild-card New York Giants, a team they'd already beaten twice in 2007. Owens had only four receptions for 49 yards and a touchdown.

After the game, he defended Romo, who had been criticized for taking a bye week vacation to Mexico with his flashy girlfriend, Jessica Simpson. Some people had wondered if the vacation distracted Romo from focusing on the Giants' game and may have contributed to the defeat.

That talk angered Owens.

"It's really unfair," he told the media after the playoff loss. "That's my quarterback, my teammate. We lost as a team."

Ten days later, Jones announced he would pay Owens a $3 million roster bonus to bring him back for a third season in 2008. No big surprise. Owens played like a multimillion dollar player in 2007. At the end of the 2008 season, however, Jones will face a tough decision. Owens will then be 35 years old. Will Jones want to sign "T.O." to another multiyear contract or even a one-year deal?

Who knows? Owens stays in remarkable shape and hasn't lost any speed. Maybe he'll be a star until he's 40. With Terrell Owens, anything is possible.

47 Too Tall and Harvey

The Cowboys had the best defensive end tandem in the league from the mid-1970s to the mid-1980s. Ed "Too Tall" Jones and Harvey Martin repeatedly stuffed runners and sacked passers. Both enjoyed long, productive careers. Martin played from 1973 to 1983, and made the Pro Bowl four times. Jones played from 1974 to 1989 (with a year off in 1979) and went to three Pro Bowls. Jones set a record for longevity. He played in more games, 224, than any other Cowboy in history.

Martin came to the Cowboys a year before Jones as a third-round pick out of East Texas State University. Martin remembers being awed by the veterans.

"I tried to keep my mind on business, yet I couldn't help but gawk," Martin wrote in his autobiography, *Texas Thunder*. "There I was, standing next to television heroes Roger Staubach, Craig Morton, Mel Renfro, Bob Lilly, Jethro Pugh. Many of them were already Super Bowl champions, and I was just a snot-nosed kid out of a jerkwater East Texas college."

Martin soon proved he belonged with his idols. He earned a starting job and began terrorizing quarterbacks. Martin, 6' 5" and 250 pounds, used his tremendous speed to blow past offensive linemen. In 10 of his 11 seasons, he led the Cowboys in sacks.

His best year was 1977 when he had 20 sacks to set a team record. He was named the NFL Defensive Player of the year and also co-Most Valuable Player in Super Bowl XII. Martin shared the award with defensive tackle Randy White after a 27–10 win over Denver.

"He was so big and so strong that he could run right past the tackles," fullback Robert Newhouse said of Martin. "He was strong and fast, and you couldn't stop him. It didn't matter how many guys you tried to put over there, he would get to the quarterback."

Despite his intensity on the field, Martin was mild-mannered and funny off the field. He hosted a radio show called *The Beautiful Harvey Martin*

Too Tall Steps into the Ring

After five years as a defensive end for the Cowboys, Ed Jones decided to make a career change. He became a professional boxer. His teammates and coaches were stunned. Jones wasn't pulling a stunt, because he'd always wanted to be a boxer.

Unlike most people with a secret ambition, Jones acted on his dream. In 1979, he stepped away from football and into the ring.

"I didn't want to be 50, look back and wish that I had pursued my lifelong dream," Jones said.

No one, including Jones, knew how he would do. Perhaps he would fail miserably. Or perhaps he would become a contender for the heavyweight crown. Jones had six professional fights against no-name opponents and won them all. He then grew disenchanted with boxing and returned to the Cowboys for the 1980 season. They were delighted to have him back. The team had never found a suitable replacement for Jones as defensive end.

Jones said the year away from football actually extended his career.

"If I hadn't boxed, there's no way I would've played 15 years in the NFL because my head wasn't there," he said. "The game is too tough. If you're not focused on football, somebody will knock your head off."

Show. "I'm still trying to live that name down," Martin once joked.

Jones, at 6' 9" and 275 pounds, was bigger than Martin. In fact, he was bigger than anyone in the league. Jones was a first-round pick in 1974 from Tennessee State, where he also starred in basketball. His towering height gave opposing quarterbacks fits as they tried to spot receivers.

"Ed was probably the most consistent guy we had," said safety Michael Downs. "Harvey would lead the team in sacks, but he seldom made tackles at the line of scrimmage because he was always in the starting block [to rush the passer]…that put Ed in position to make a lot of plays."

When Jimmy Johnson became coach in 1989, he pressured several long-time veterans to retire. Jones, for one, resisted. He wanted to keep playing. Johnson developed a deep appreciation for the longtime veteran, who retired at the end of the season.

"Ed Jones, of all the players I have ever worked with, is the one who truly said 'professional,'" Johnson wrote in his autobiography. "He truly approached it as a job. And he truly approached you as his employer. I really enjoyed working with him, even at the end of his career. I would have loved to have coached Ed Jones when he was in his prime."

After retiring, Jones had a successful business career. Martin, by contrast, had a string of business failures. He also battled drug addiction. In his autobiography, he admits to using cocaine in 1980 while still playing.

"It took over my life to the point where I was not myself," Martin wrote. "I really didn't like the person I saw in the mirror, but I didn't know how to change it. I didn't know how to stop."

Martin died in 2001 of pancreatic cancer at the age 51. Teammates praised him as a person and a player. Defensive end Jim Jeffcoat, who was a rookie in Martin's last season, said Martin took a special interest in him.

"Harvey taught me a lot about the game and how to be a professional," Jeffcoat said. "He prepared me to follow him and … I was always appreciative of that."

Charles Haley

Charles Haley had a short career as a Cowboy, but he made a huge impact. The Cowboys acquired the defensive end in a trade from the San Francisco 49ers in 1992. The 49ers were ready to unload him. Although Haley was a ferocious pass rusher, he created problems in the locker room with his surly attitude and criticism of coaches.

The Cowboys thought they could handle Haley. They needed a big-time playmaker on the defensive line, and Haley was certainly that. In 1990, he was been the NFC Defensive Player of the Year after recording 16 sacks. In his six years with the 49ers, Haley had an astounding 63.5 sacks and helped the team win two Super Bowls.

"Charles Haley was the premier pass rusher in the league," coach Jimmy Johnson wrote in his autobiography. "We'd been busy shoring up our secondary, but if we could get Haley in the defensive front for passing situations, that would be a leap in our pass defense that we hadn't anticipated."

Owner Jerry Jones swapped a second-round pick in 1993 and a third-rounder in 1994 for Haley. It turned out to be a steal. After he joined the Cowboys, Haley immediately became the team's best pass rusher, and the entire defense improved. At 6' 5" and 255 pounds, he had a unique combination of speed, quickness and strength. In addition, Haley had a mean, street-fighting attitude that the still-developing Cowboys desperately needed.

It's no coincidence the Cowboys won three Super Bowls after Haley arrived. He had outstanding regular seasons and even better post-seasons. In Super Bowl XXVII, Haley made a huge hit on Buffalo quarterback Jim Kelly in the first quarter, forcing him to fumble. Defensive lineman Jimmie Jones picked up the ball and ran in for a touchdown to give Dallas a 14–7 lead. The Cowboys never relinquished the lead en route to a 52–17 blowout.

In the NFC Championship Game the following season, the Cowboys faced the 49ers. Haley had an outstanding performance against his old team, with a sack, a forced fumble, and a deflected pass. The Cowboys won, 38–21. "This was my Super Bowl," Haley said afterward.

Two weeks later, in Super Bowl XXVIII, the Cowboys rolled over the Bills, 30–13. Haley had another strong outing. In 1994, the Cowboys lost to the 49ers in the NFC Championship Game, missing out on a chance to win three straight Super Bowls although Haley had 12.5 sacks during the regular season to lead the team, and also forced more fumbles than any other player. The next year, Haley and the Cowboys were determined to win another ring. He missed the last three games because of back surgery, and most people thought Haley was done for the year. Instead, he returned in the playoffs. Haley had a sack, three quarterback pressures, and five tackles in the Cowboys' 27–17 win over Pittsburgh in Super Bowl XXX.

Throughout his career, Haley had a volatile temper and rarely talked to the press. In 1993, Emmitt Smith missed the first two games in a contract holdout. The Cowboys lost both games. Rookie Derrick Lassic, Smith's replacement, fumbled twice in the second loss.

"We're never going to win with this rookie running back," Haley fumed in the locker room.

His outburst, perhaps, prompted owner Jerry Jones to sweeten his contract offer to Smith and sign him before the next game. Late in the 1995 season, as the Cowboys were looking to the playoffs, Haley spoke his mind again. He openly criticized the defensive coaching staff, but the brass let his comments slide. They had learned that Haley would erupt from time to time. On game day, he made big plays and that was all that mattered to them.

Haley retired from the Cowboys after the 1996 season. The next year, he wrote an autobiography titled, *All the Rage: The Life of an NFL Renegade.*

The title couldn't be more appropriate.

49 Super Bowl Losses to Steelers

Cowboys' safety Cliff Harris has many good memories from his 10-year career. But don't ask him to recall the team's two Super Bowl losses to the Pittsburgh Steelers in the mid-1970s. Both were narrow, bitter defeats that dogged the Cowboys for years.

"I don't like to talk or even think about our Pittsburgh Super Bowls," Harris wrote in *Tales from the Dallas Cowboys.* "The Steelers were a very good team, but I feel we could, and should, have beaten them in both of those Super Bowls."

In Super Bowl X, after the 1975 season, the Steelers beat the Cowboys, 21–17. In Super Bowl XIII, the Steelers won again, 35–31. In both games, Dallas had chances to win.

The Cowboys lead 10–7 at halftime of Super Bowl X, thanks to a 29-yard touchdown pass by Roger Staubach and a 36-yard field goal. Dallas held onto the slim lead through the third quarter. In the fourth, the Steelers scored 14 unanswered points to take a 21–10 lead. The last touchdown came on a 64-yard pass to wide receiver Lynn Swann, who killed the

Cowboys all day. He had four spectacular, acrobatic catches for a Super Bowl record 161 yards receiving.

Staubach threw a 34-yard touchdown late in the fourth quarter to make the score 21–17. The Cowboys later stopped the Steelers on fourth down and got the ball back with 1:22 remaining. Staubach ran and passed for two first downs, and a miracle comeback seemed possible. Dallas had moved to the Steelers' 38-yard line with 22 seconds left. But Staubach threw an incompletion and had another pass batted down. On his final attempt, he threw an interception in the end zone. Pittsburgh held on to win.

The ending was disappointing, but no one had expected the Cowboys to be in the Super Bowl. They were coming off a season in which they had missed the playoffs for the first time in almost a decade. The 1975 season was expected to be devoted to rebuilding. The roster included a dozen rookies, nicknamed the Dirty Dozen. The players included future stars Thomas Hollywood Henderson, Randy White, and Bob Breunig. The young and old players coalesced and produced a 10–4 record, good enough for a wild-card playoff spot. The Cowboys became the first wild-card team to advance to the Super Bowl.

In 1978, the Cowboys had an even stronger team. They finished 12–4 and won the NFC East. They swept past Atlanta and Los Angeles in the playoffs to meet the Steelers for a rematch in Super Bowl XIII. Fans anticipated an exciting game, and they weren't disappointed. Pittsburgh scored first on a 28-yard pass from Terry Bradshaw to John Stallworth only five minutes into the game. Stallworth scored again on a 75-yard touchdown pass early in the second quarter. He was having the kind of spectacular day his teammate Swann enjoyed in Super Bowl X.

Dallas, meanwhile, had scored on a 39-yard touchdown pass and a 37-yard fumble return and trailed 21–14 at halftime. In the third quarter, Dallas held the Steelers scoreless and kicked a 27-yard field goal to close the gap to 21–17.

In the fourth quarter, the Pittsburgh offense caught fire again. The Steelers scored two touchdowns and widened their lead to 35–17. Dallas then mounted a furious comeback. Quarterback Roger Staubach, Captain Comeback, threw a 7-yard touchdown pass to tight end Billy Joe DuPree with less than 3 minutes remaining.

After recovering an onside kick, the Cowboys went to work again. Staubach connected with receiver Butch Johnson on a 4-yard TD pass. But the comeback was too little, too late. Only 22 seconds remained after the last touchdown, and the Cowboys never got the ball back. Pittsburgh won, 35–31.

The Cowboys were haunted by a missed touchdown opportunity in the third quarter that could have changed the game. Dallas tight end Jackie Smith, who had come out of retirement to join the Cowboys in 1978, dropped a 10-yard pass in the end zone. Smith was all alone, and Staubach carefully lobbed the ball to him. It was a little behind him, but still able to be caught. Smith, however, lost his footing as he reached back for the ball. It bounced off his chest and hit the ground.

A famous photo shot seconds later shows Smith lying on the ground, his eyes closed and fists clenched. He is grimacing as if in pain.

"I never saw a more despondent player than Jackie Smith in the locker room following Super Bowl XIII," coach Tom Landry said. "Jackie felt absolutely sick. And I felt for him."

Staubach never blamed Smith. Instead, he faulted himself for throwing the ball behind him. "I've gone over that pass to Smith time and time again," Staubach said.

Smith came to the Cowboys after a 15-year, All-Pro career with the St. Louis Cardinals. He had never been to a Super Bowl before and desperately wanted to win. In the years since the loss, Smith has lived with the pain of the drop. In Super Bowl XXX, a new generation of Cowboys and Steelers met again for the NFL title.

Naturally, reporters wanted to ask Smith about the infamous dropped pass. He didn't want to discuss it.

"I think 17 years is enough to be nice, and I don't want to be nice about it anymore," Smith said.

End of interview.

50 Super Bowl XII

The 1977 Cowboys were one of the best teams in club history. They compiled a 12–2 record that included a 37–0 shellacking of the Detroit Lions. The Cowboys also beat division foes Washington, Philadelphia, and New York twice each.

Tony Dorsett, the team's No. 1 draft choice, rushed for 1,007 yards and scored 12 touchdowns as a rookie. The roster also included battle-tested veterans Roger Staubach and Drew Pearson. In the playoffs, the Cowboys easily rolled over Chicago, 37–7, and Minnesota, 23–6, to face the Denver Broncos in Super Bowl XII.

It was an intriguing match up. Denver was led by quarterback Craig Morton, a former No. 1 draft pick of the Cowboys who had been traded after he lost his starting job to Staubach. Morton initially went to the New York Giants and then to Denver, where he was named NFL Comeback Player of the Year in 1977.

Few expected Denver to make it to the Super Bowl. In the playoffs, they defeated the Pittsburgh Steelers and the Oakland Raiders, the defending Super Bowl champs. Denver relied heavily on its Orange Crush defense, which featured defensive end Lyle Alzado and linebackers Randy Gradishar and Tom Jackson.

The Cowboys were listed as a five-point favorite, but they weren't overconfident. They had suffered a stinging 21–17 loss to Pittsburgh two years earlier in Super Bowl X. In the first half, the Cowboys dominated. Dorsett scored on a 3-yard touchdown run, and Efren Herrera added two field goals to give Dallas a 13–0 halftime lead.

Early in the third quarter, Denver kicked a 47-yard field goal to narrow the gap to 13–3. Dallas, however, quickly scored on a 45-yard touchdown pass from Staubach to receiver Butch Johnson. Johnson made a remarkable diving catch as he crossed the goal line. He laid out parallel to the ground and caught the ball in his fingertips.

The touchdown gave the Cowboys a commanding 20–3 lead. Denver's Rob Lytle scored on a 1-yard run late in the third quarter to make the score 20–10, but Dallas still had control of the game. In the fourth quarter, the Cowboys ran a trick play that surprised everyone. Fullback Robert Newhouse took a pitch and began running around the end. He then stopped and tossed a perfect pass to receiver Golden Richards. He nabbed it and scored a 29-yard touchdown.

Dallas held Denver and won 27–10 in dominating fashion. The Cowboys had 325 yards of total offense, compared with only 156 for Denver. Staubach was brilliant, completing 17 of 25 passes with no interceptions. Morton, meanwhile, had a miserable day. He threw a Super Bowl record four first-half interceptions before being yanked.

Denver's famed defense didn't rise to the occasion. Instead, Dallas' defense dominated with four fumble recoveries and four interceptions. The defense included stalwarts Ed "Too Tall" Jones and Jethro Pugh on the line, and Cliff Harris and Charlie Waters in the secondary. The Cowboys' two All-Pro linemen, Randy White and Harvey Martin, were named co-Most Valuable Players. It was the first time two players shared the award.

Super Bowl XII marked Dallas' second championship of the 1970s. They returned the next year in Super Bowl XIII, but the outcome wouldn't be so favorable.

51 Redskins Rivalry

Intense rivalries aren't unusual in the NFL, but few have the tradition and bitterness of the Cowboys-Redskins feud. The bad blood developed in the early 1970s when George Allen took over as Washington coach. Before that, the Cowboys and Redskins disliked each other. After all, they were division rivals who played each other twice a year. But Allen ratcheted up the hostility to a new level.

He seemed to genuinely hate the Cowboys—the players, the coaches, the entire organization. He wasn't just putting on an act. He imparted his hatred to his team and even the fans at Washington's RFK Stadium.

"The fans in RFK hated the Cowboys," Dallas safety Cliff Harris said. "There were only 55,000 of them, but it was such a closed stadium, the sound reverberated. I've often said if they would have let the gates down, and said it was okay to kill the Cowboys, the fans would have killed the Cowboys."

Allen joined the Redskins in 1971 after five years with the Los Angeles Rams. He had succeeded there, taking a perennial loser and turning it into a winner. In 1967, he was named NFL Coach of the Year after leading the Rams to an 11–1–2 record.

With the Redskins, Allen faced an even bigger rebuilding task. Washington had only one winning season in the previous 15 years. In his first year, Allen began to work his magic. The Redskins' record shot to 9–4–1. The next year, the Redskins improved to 11–3, beat Dallas in the NFC Championship Game and met the Miami Dolphins in Super Bowl VII. The Dolphins won, 14–7.

Allen had immediate success with the Redskins, because he traded future draft picks for time-tested veterans. He didn't have the patience to build a team through the draft. "The future is now," Allen liked to say.

He was a true workaholic.

"Leisure is the five or six hours you sleep each night," he would say. "Every day you waste is one you can't make up."

Before Allen arrived, the Cowboys routinely dominated the Redskins. Dallas had won six straight games over Washington. But in Allen's first game against the Cowboys, the Redskins won, 20–16.

"Dallas had a lot more talent than we did," Redskins quarterback Billy Kilmer said. "We beat them on emotion and hard play."

During Allen's seven seasons in Washington, the Redskins and Cowboys regularly played close games that often decided the division title. The match-up was particularly interesting because of the dramatically different personalities of the coaches. Allen fired up his players with emotional pep talks. Landry relied on preparation and precision.

"George could motivate a team," Redskins fullback Charley Harraway said. "We had a bunch of veterans, and we would look at each other when George was giving one of his rah-rah talks. We would be smiling and jumping around the room like little kids. It was corny, but it was fun."

Lineman Diron Talbert, who enjoyed trash talking himself, said Allen sometimes used bizarre tactics.

"We'd be sitting in a Jacuzzi, and he'd come in and get in that crouched position and say, 'We're going to get that Staubach and ring his neck!'" Talbert said.

Washington briefly had a defensive end named Dallas Hickman. Allen refused to call him by his first name. He wouldn't even refer to the "Dallas" Cowboys, said Washington general manager Charley Casserly.

"He would call them the 'damn Cowboys,'" he said. "If you lost to Dallas, it was like the end of the world."

In 1977, the Redskins finished 9–5. Despite producing seven straight winning seasons, Allen was fired. After he left, the Dallas-Washington rivalry cooled for a few years. But it resumed, with a slightly different character, when Joe Gibbs became coach in 1981. He was much more like Landry, quiet and efficient.

Under Gibbs, the Redskins became a dominant team. They won three Super Bowls during his 11 years in Washington. The Redskins' rise in the 1980s coincided with the Cowboys' decline. Still, the Cowboys always managed to play well against the Redskins.

In the 1990s, the Cowboys returned to greatness, while the Redskins dipped. But the Redskins, like the Cowboys had done earlier, always played their best against Dallas.

There's an old football cliché that's used when two bitter rivals meet. "Throw out the records."

Translation: Regardless of the standings, either team can win. The cliché certainly applies to the Cowboys-Redskins battles.

52 The Best Redskins Game

The Cowboys and Redskins have played many thrilling games over the past five decades. None top Dallas' amazing 35–34 win on December 16, 1979, at Texas Stadium.

Quarterback Roger Staubach was playing his last regular-season game after an illustrious 11-year career. If the Cowboys won, they would finish 11–5 and claim the division title. By winning, they could also knock the Redskins out of playoff contention, providing extra motivation.

The Redskins stunned the Cowboys by taking a 17–0 lead early in the second quarter. But the Cowboys, with Staubach at the helm, never gave up. Dallas scored three straight touchdowns to pull in front, 21–17. Then the momentum swung back to Washington. The Redskins scored three fourth-quarter touchdowns to take a seemingly comfortable 34–21 lead. Only 6:54 remained in the game.

Then the fun began. Dallas defensive tackle Randy White recovered a Washington fumble at the Cowboys' 41-yard line. Staubach drove the team steadily down the field, finally throwing a 26-yard touchdown pass to full-back Ron Springs. The gap narrowed to 34–28 with only 2:20 left. A Dallas win still seemed unlikely.

The Redskins got the ball back and planned to run out the clock. But they needed to make a first down on third-and-2. All-Pro running back John Riggins, who already had 153 yards rushing and two touchdowns, took the handoff. Dallas defensive tackle Larry Cole broke through the Washington line and tackled Riggins for a 2-yard loss. The Redskins had to punt, and the Cowboys began their final drive at their 25-yard line. Only 1:46 remained.

On first down, Staubach hit receiver Tony Hill for 20 yards. Two plays later, Staubach connected with Preston Pearson for 22 yards. He found Pearson again for 25 yards. Now the Cowboys were at the Washington 8-yard line with only 45 seconds left.

On first and goal, Staubach threw an incomplete pass to Hill. On the next play, the Redskins called a blitz. Staubach retreated to avoid the rush, and spotted Hill running toward the corner of the end zone. He lofted the ball over Hill's shoulder, and he made the catch. Final score: Dallas 35, Washington 34.

"We just never quit," Staubach said. "It was absolutely the most thrilling 60 minutes I ever spent on a football field."

Redskin cornerback Lemar Parrish said Staubach threw a perfect pass. "It was the pass that beat me," he said. "There's nothing you can do to stop it."

The loss gave the Redskins a 10–6 record, normally good enough to make the playoffs. But because of a complex tiebreaker system, the Redskins found themselves out of the postseason. If they had won, they would have taken the division title.

"We went from being division champs to the outhouse," Washington coach Jack Pardee said.

Some of the Cowboys didn't initially know they had knocked the Redskins out of the playoffs.

"When we found out about it, we said, 'Hey, that's great,'" said defensive back Benny Barnes. "They deserved it."

53 Legal Troubles

Pro football players can make terrible role models. Some play well on the field, but conduct themselves poorly off the field. The Cowboys may be America's Team, but their players have had plenty of run-ins with the law.

The incidents go back to the early days of the franchise. In 1970, for instance, star wide receiver Lance Rentzel was arrested for indecent exposure. He exposed himself to a young girl in Highland Park, an affluent Dallas suburb, and someone took down his license plate number.

Rentzel immediately quit the team. He pled guilty and was given five years of probation. The incident shocked the town and his teammates. It was the first highly publicized arrest of a Cowboy, and seemed to make no sense. Rentzel was a young, good-looking star with a beautiful wife, actress Joey Heatherton.

"The humiliation crushed me," Rentzel wrote in a book about the incident, *When All the Laughter Died in Sorrow*. "I had ruined my reputation and my career. I had destroyed my marriage and driven away the only woman I'd ever really loved."

The year after his arrest, the Cowboys traded Rentzel to the Los Angeles Rams. He had several productive seasons before retiring in 1974. Years later, he said he took full responsibility for his arrest, but regretted that he couldn't finish his career as a Cowboy.

"You can never get away from something like that," Rentzel said. "What you can do is become a better person, treat people right, and own up to your mistakes. You don't make them again, and I haven't."

John Niland, an All-Pro guard in the 1960s and '70s, was the next Cowboy to have an arrest that made headlines. In 1973, police responded to a call that Niland was running down a residential street at night in a crazed state. He knocked on someone's door, and the frightened person called the police. Eventually, it took seven officers to subdue Niland. They took him to a nearby hospital for a psychiatric exam.

In the scuffle, Niland injured his elbow and suffered nerve damage in his hand. He was placed on injured reserve for the rest of the 1974 season, then traded to the Philadelphia Eagles before the 1975 season. He played another year and retired.

Many years later, Niland discussed the bizarre incident. He said he thought he was possessed by the devil. He said the experience led to a religious conversion.

"The Lord smacked me right on the face, got my attention," Niland said.

In the late 1970s, Thomas "Hollywood" Henderson was one of the top linebackers in football. He also was a drug addict. He admitted as much in his 1987 book, *Out of Control: Confessions of an NFL Casualty*. He wrote that he snorted cocaine on the sidelines during Super Bowl XIII. He avoided arrest as a player, but in 1984 he was convicted of another charge:

having sex with an underage girl he met at a drug party. Henderson served more than two years in prison.

In the late 1970s and early 1980s, Rafael Septien was a star kicker, the best in Cowboys' history. But his career came to an abrupt halt in early 1987. Septien was indicted for sexually assaulting a 10-year-old girl, the daughter of a friend. Septien maintained his innocence, but the Cowboys released him.

In the 1990s and beyond, current and former Cowboy players had a rash of legal problems. All-Pro receiver Michael Irvin was arrested on cocaine possession charges in 1996. Sherman Williams, a former running back, was sentenced to 15 years in prison in 2001 for drug trafficking and counterfeiting. Nate Newton, a former offensive lineman, spent from 2001 to 2004 in federal prison for selling drugs.

In 2003, former defensive back Dwayne Goodrich was convicted of criminally negligent homicide. After leaving a Dallas strip club late at night, Goodrich struck and killed two men who had stopped to help a motorist on a freeway. He also injured a third man before leaving the scene in his BMW.

Goodrich originally received a seven-year sentence, but a judge later added five years to Goodrich's sentence for failing to stop and render aid. At Goodrich's trial, the injured man said he forgave the former Cowboy.

"I don't hate him," he said. "I feel sorry for him."

54 Read *North Dallas Forty*

Pete Gent had a forgettable career as a Cowboy receiver. He played from 1964 to 1968, mostly as a backup. Gent turned his experiences into a best-selling 1973 novel, *North Dallas Forty*.

It didn't glorify the Cowboys and professional football. Instead, its message was that pro football is strictly business, and that management can be ruthless in dealing with players. In the book, coaches urge injured players to take painkillers so they can perform, even though they're risking greater long-term injury. The book has plenty of humor, too. It describes the crazy partying, drinking, and womanizing of star athletes of Gent's era. Little may have changed since.

Members of the Dallas Cowboys organization were shocked when *North Dallas Forty* hit the stands and contained thinly veiled references to the Cowboys. For instance, the quarterback, a fun-loving guy named Seth Maxwell, was a dead ringer for Don Meredith. The coach, a strict, humorless man named B.A. Strothers, was undoubtedly Tom Landry.

Is the book accurate? Its message is heavy-handed, and the characters—particularly the Landry character—are exaggerated stereotypes. Still, the book's essence is true: Football is a business. *North Dallas Forty* is probably most accurate in its portrayal of the athletes' personal lives. Many are wild, immature men used to being worshipped as gods. The players drink excessively, smoke dope, and enjoy sexual escapades with beautiful women.

The book is right, certainly, in capturing the fear of pro athletes. They're afraid an injury will end their career, or they'll make a few bad plays and be cut. Because of fear, the players abuse their bodies to try to keep going. Phil Elliott, a character based on Gent's career, relies on painkillers to suit up each week. He has a bum knee that causes him to limp, but an injection on game day lets him take the field.

"It's like a brand new knee," Elliott said after a shot. "Better football through chemistry."

The film version of *North Dallas Forty*, which came out in 1979, stays true to the novel. Mac Davis, a country singing star in the 1970s, plays Maxwell, the quarterback. Nick Nolte plays Elliott. They're believable as football stars and as close friends. An NFL player of the day, John Matuszak, has a minor role as a juiced-up, crazed lineman.

The Nolte character is the most complex, conflicted in the novel. In a way, he wants to quit the game because it's wrecking his body. But he can't walk away because he loves the high he gets from competing. Elliott realizes, and accepts, that owners and coaches want players who will shut up, play hurt, and not buck the system.

"What's important is the moment of the catch," Elliott says. "That feeling, that high. Hell, I can take the crap. I can take the manipulation. I can take the pain. As long as I get that chance every Sunday."

North Dallas Forty may have been written 35 years ago, and its message may be simplistic in parts. But it still offers valuable insight into the minds of players and management.

55 Lee Roy Jordan

Lee Roy Jordan patrolled the middle of the Dallas defense for 14 years. He was undersized for a middle linebacker, weighing only 215 pounds. Jordan made up for his lack of size with tenacity and hustle. No one worked harder or prepared more than Jordan.

He became the defense's leader. If he thought a teammate needed a butt kicking, he'd administer it.

"Lee Roy was a holler guy, always full of fire, tough as steel," defensive end Harvey Martin wrote in his autobiography, *Texas Thunder*. "Lee Roy never gave up, and he was a terrific hitter. He could break a leg and still come limping after you on the other."

Jordan played during the same era as Dick Butkus, the 6' 3" and 245-pound beast of a middle linebacker for the Chicago Bears.

"If Jordan weighed as much as Dick Butkus, they'd have to outlaw him from football," Cowboys' defensive coach Ernie Stautner once said.

Jordan was the Cowboys' No. 1 pick in 1963, and the sixth overall in the draft. He played under legendary coach Paul Bear Bryant at Alabama and earned All American honors as a senior. The Crimson Tide won the national championship in Jordan's sophomore year, and the team lost only two games during his three years.

"He would have made every tackle on every play if they had stayed in bounds," Bryant wrote in his autobiography. "I never had another one like Lee Roy Jordan."

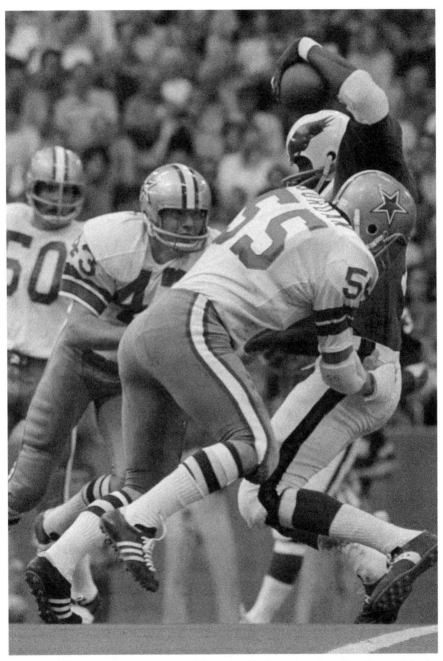

Lee Roy Jordan and teammates swarm Philadelphia Eagles wide receiver Harold Carmichael during a November 1971 game.

Jordan grew up in the tiny farming community of Excel, Alabama. He loved playing for Bryant.

"He used to use a lot of guys who were smaller in stature because he wanted quickness, pursuit, and endurance," Jordan said. "He was hard and demanding, but he always knew how to put that arm on your shoulder and get you to do some more."

As a Dallas rookie, Jordan played outside linebacker, missing the second half of the season with a kidney injury. In his second year, he earned a starting job at middle linebacker and didn't relinquish it until he retired in 1976. He was part of the original Doomsday Defense that included outside linebacker Chuck Howley and tackles Bob Lilly and Jethro Pugh.

Jordan played in the two classic championship games against the Green Bay Packers in 1966 and 1967. Dallas narrowly lost both games. In the latter, Green Bay won, 21–17, on a last-second quarterback sneak by Bart Starr. The game became known as the Ice Bowl because of the frigid conditions—13 degrees below zero at kickoff.

Jordan also played in the Cowboys' disappointing 16–13 loss to the Baltimore Colts in Super Bowl V. The Cowboys committed four turnovers and fell on a last-second field goal.

"The lowest we had ever been was after we had lost to Baltimore in Super Bowl V," Jordan said.

The next year, he and his teammates routed the Miami Dolphins, 24–3, in Super Bowl VI. Miami had a potent running game that featured three outstanding backs, Larry Csonka, Mercury Morris, and Jim Kiick. They had averaged 174 yards a game rushing.

But in the Super Bowl, Jordan and the Dallas defense held the Miami backs to only 80 yards. On the Dolphins' second possession, Jordan helped force a Csonka fumble that Dallas recovered near midfield. The Cowboys quickly grabbed a 3–0 lead and never looked back.

During his 14-year career, Jordan was named to the Pro Bowl five times. He had 32 interceptions, including three in one game in 1973. He also had 18 fumble recoveries. He retired after the 1976 season, even though he enjoyed one of his best years.

"I was 36 years old and had played 14 years," Jordan said. "For a guy who was supposed to be too small to play, I had a miracle career."

56 Chuck Howley

Chuck Howley's career almost ended after only one year. The Chicago Bears drafted Howley with their No. 1 choice in 1958. He started as a rookie, but suffered a serious knee injury early in 1959, missing the rest of the season. The Bears then released him.

Howley returned to his native West Virginia, bought a gas station, and began running it. "It was an available business that I knew a little bit about," he said.

He didn't own the business long. In 1961, Cowboys' general manager Tex Schramm asked if Howley would like to play for the young team. Howley wasn't sure if his knee would let him resume his career, but he wanted to try.

The knee turned out to be fine, and Howley quickly became a star. He made the Pro Bowl in 1965, the first of six selections. Howley, 6' 3" and 230 pounds, became an integral part of the Doomsday Defense of late 1960s and early 1970s.

Howley played in the Ice Bowl, the infamous 1967 NFL Championship between Dallas and Green Bay. At kickoff, the temperature was 13 below, and it dropped during the game. The Packers won, 21–17, on a Bart Starr quarterback sneak with only 16 seconds remaining.

"I was laying on Bart Starr's back as he went across," Howley said. "We were keying the fullback, Jim Taylor. It didn't happen, and they got the surge off the line of scrimmage, and that's all you need on a quarterback sneak because the ball was on the one-inch line."

Howley had been an all-around athlete at the University of West Virginia. He lettered in five sports: football, track, gymnastics, wrestling, and diving.

"When I went out for gymnastics at the university, the coach remarked, 'What's this big dumb guy going to be able to do?'" Howley said. "He found out quickly enough I could compete on the college level."

Howley relied on his speed and agility to consistently make big plays in the NFL. In 1966, he returned a fumble 97 yards for a touchdown against the Falcons. He had one of his best games in Super Bowl V. Howley intercepted two passes and recovered a fumble. He was named the game's Most Valuable Player, even though the Cowboys fell to the Baltimore Colts, 16–13.

"It was hard to rejoice," Howley said of the award. "We had just lost the biggest game of the season."

In Super Bowl VI the next year, Howley again played well. Early in the fourth quarter, he intercepted a pass near midfield. He seemed to have a clear path to a touchdown, but he fell at the 9-yard line without ever being touched.

"Nobody around me, blockers everywhere, and I just crash," Howley said. "Needless to say, it was a little embarrassing. At that particular moment, I was wishing it had been a very deep hole I had fallen into."

His embarrassment was eased by the fact that the Cowboys crushed the Dolphins, 24–3, to win their first world championship. "After losing to Baltimore, there was a fixation with everyone to win the Super Bowl," Howley said. "In the first one, we questioned whether we should be there. That season, we didn't have any doubt."

Howley played two more years, retiring after the 1973 season. He finished his career with 25 interceptions, including six in 1968. He also recovered 18 fumbles in his career. He earned the respect of coach Tom Landry and was one of the first players inducted into the Cowboys' Ring of Honor in 1976.

"I don't know that I've ever seen anybody better at linebacker than Howley," Landry said.

57 Mel Renfro

Mel Renfro was inducted into the Pro Football Hall of Fame in 1996, a great honor, but one that came much too late. He retired in 1977 with 52 interceptions, a Cowboys record that still stands. He made the Pro Bowl 10 times. Many of his teammates believe Renfro should have made the Hall of Fame in 1982, his first year of eligibility.

During his 14-year career, opposing quarterbacks rarely challenged Renfro.

"They wouldn't throw at him because he always intercepted it or knocked it down," defensive tackle Bob Lilly said.

The Cowboys drafted Renfro with their second pick in 1964. He had been a two-time All-American running back at Oregon, as well as an outstanding sprinter, long jumper, and hurdler. The Cowboys immediately converted Renfro to defense. At 6' and 190 pounds, he wasn't big enough to take a weekly pounding at running back.

Renfro excelled at safety. He started as a rookie and intercepted seven passes, returning one for a touchdown. He also led the NFL in kickoff and punt return yardage. The league selected him Rookie of the Year.

In 1965, Renfro's second year, he returned an interception 90 yards for a touchdown and a kickoff of 100 yards. He came to the Cowboys as they began to develop into a consistent winner. In his rookie year, Dallas finished 5–8–1. The next year, they were 7–7. Beginning in 1966, the Cowboys made the playoffs eight straight years. "There were a lot of good times," Renfro said.

Renfro played in the two championship losses to the Green Bay Packers in 1966 and 1967. He'd rather forget the first game. He fumbled a kickoff early in the opening quarter, and the Packers ran in for a touchdown to take a 14–0 lead. The Packers won, 34–27.

Renfro also played in Super Bowl V. Renfro was involved in a freak play that helped turn the game in Baltimore's favor. Colts quarterback Johnny Unitas threw a pass to receiver Eddie Hinton, who tipped the ball in Renfro's direction. It then fell into the arms of tight end John Mackey, who ran 75 yards for a touchdown.

The play was controversial because Renfro denied touching the ball. According to the rules, one offensive player couldn't tip the ball to a teammate unless a defender touched the ball in between. If the officials had ruled Renfro didn't touch the ball, the touchdown would not have counted. Baltimore won, 16–13, on a last-second field goal.

After the Super Bowl loss, Renfro played in the 1971 Pro Bowl. He had a remarkable game, returning two punts for touchdowns in leading the NFC to a 27–6 win. He was named the Most Valuable Player. "That day took some of the sting out of the disappointment of losing the Super Bowl," Renfro said.

The next year, he and the Cowboys vindicated themselves with a 24–3 pounding of the Miami Dolphins in Super Bowl VI. "That was a team thing, something we had all worked long and hard for," Renfro said.

He played in two other Super Bowls—a 21–17 loss to Pittsburgh in Super Bowl X and a 27–10 victory over Denver in Super Bowl XII.

Renfro made contributions off the field, too. In the late 1960s, Dallas was still largely segregated. Even prominent blacks, such as Renfro, couldn't find housing in the more affluent areas of North Dallas. After being denied a townhouse lease in 1968, Renfro filed a federal lawsuit against the developer. He won the suit, and he and his family moved in.

"I opened the door for a lot of people," Renfro said. "I got a lot of positive mail from people of color that said because of what I had done, they could live where they wanted."

In 1981, the Cowboys inducted Renfro into the team's Ring of Honor. In 1996, he went into the Pro Football Hall of Fame, 14 years after he was originally eligible.

"I can honestly say I wasn't sure I would make the Hall of Fame," he said in his acceptance speech. "Now, I've made it at the last second. I'm so very thankful."

58 Cornell Green

Cornell Green made a remarkably quick transition from college basketball star to cornerback in the NFL. Green didn't even play football at Utah State. The Cowboys offered him a free agent contract based on his athletic ability and potential.

Team officials liked Green's size, 6' 4" and 211 pounds, and thought he could develop into an excellent football player. They were right. He started as a rookie in 1962 and soon developed into one of the best cornerbacks in the league. He made five trips to the Pro Bowl, the last in 1972 after he moved to strong safety.

During the 1960s, the Cowboys offered several athletes free agent contracts who didn't play college football. They included Pete Gent, a basketball player who became a receiver, and Richmond Flowers, a track star who also became a receiver.

"One of the things I did was go after great athletes," general manager Tex Schramm said. "I especially wanted a star basketball player who fell in the gray area of not being tall enough to make it as a forward in the NBA, and not being quick enough to be a guard."

Green, who played high school football, said he was surprised that Schramm invited him to training camp. He wasn't sure Schramm was serious until he offered Green a bonus to show up. He could keep it even if he didn't make the team. "It was the bonus I was going for," Green said.

He did more than collect the money. He immediately impressed coaches with his football instincts and began a long career.

"You have to understand that even though I had never played college football, training camp gave you plenty of time to learn what you needed to know," Green said. "For me, playing defensive back under Tom Landry's system was easy, because back in those days, 90 percent of the time it was just 'man' coverage. We didn't have a lot of zones and combinations."

Green led the team in interceptions four times and retired in 1975 with 34 picks. He may have dropped almost that many. His teammates nick-named him Boards because he had trouble holding onto the ball.

While he was still playing, Green also worked as a scout for the Cowboys in the off season, helping to spot promising talent. He's been a fulltime scout for other teams since he retired.

"I scouted some of the kids' dads and now I'm scouting their sons," Green said. "It's just a lot more technical now than it was when I first started with the Cowboys. There's more psychological testing and all that type of stuff. Everybody's got a different test that they give kids to see if they can play football."

The Cowboys didn't need any fancy testing to know that Green could play. All they had to do was watch a few practices back in 1962. Green's talent became clear to them and, soon, to many other people as well.

59 Calvin Hill

The Cowboys made Calvin Hill their No. 1 draft choice in 1969. He'd been an outstanding running back at Yale, but the Cowboys weren't sure they wanted him to play in the backfield.

Coaches tried him at tight end and linebacker. At 6' 3" and 225 pounds, Hill was a natural athlete. He probably could have starred at those positions and others as well. But before the end of Hill's first training camp, coaches decided to let him run the ball.

They made a good decision. Hill rushed for 942 yards, second-most in the league. He averaged 4.6 yards per carry, and was named NFL Rookie of the Year in a landslide vote. Ironically, 23 other NFL teams passed on Hill before he landed with the Cowboys. They questioned the competition he faced in the Ivy League.

What teams should have realized is that Hill, with his size, power, and

Calvin Hill, the Dallas Cowboys' NFL Rookie of the Year in 1969, watches the Cowboys' chances for a win slip away during the waning moments of the playoff game against Cleveland on December 29, 1969.

speed, could have played at any college. In fact, he turned down scholarship offers from Notre Dame, Michigan, and UCLA to attend Yale. He liked its academic tradition. Hill starred in football and track, setting school records in the long jump and triple jump.

In his first game as a starter, Hill proved he belonged in the NFL. He rushed for 106 yards against the San Francisco 49ers in a preseason game, despite having a major case of butterflies. "I was so nervous, you would have thought I was going to the electric chair," Hill said. "There was pressure because I was the first-round draft pick, and I didn't want to be the guy from Yale who flubbed."

In the locker room, Hill received the game ball for his performance. "Today a star was born," general manager Tex Schramm said.

In his second year, Hill was plagued by injuries and missed four games. His rushing total dropped to 577 yards. His carries also were reduced by the arrival of No. 1 draft pick Duane Thomas, another immensely talented back. In 1971, Hill's third year, he again shared time with Thomas and rushed for only 468 yards.

In 1972, Hill had the job all to himself again. The Cowboys traded Thomas, tired of his grumbling and contract demands, and Hill returned to his rookie form. He rushed for 1,036 yards, becoming the first Cowboy to pass the 1,000-yard mark. In 1973, Hill had an even better year, gaining 1,142 yards.

In 1974, Hill shocked Cowboy officials by signing with the upstart World Football League. It was all about money. Hill was frustrated by his $25,000 salary in Dallas. Schramm, notoriously stingy with the payroll, had refused to renegotiate Hill's three-year contract after his outstanding rookie year.

When the WFL folded less than a year later, Hill signed with the Washington Redskins. He couldn't crack the starting lineup, but became a valuable pass receiver on third downs. After two years with Washington, Hill signed with Cleveland and played four more years. His role was primarily the same: third-down pass receiving back.

Ironically, Hill wound up back with the Cowboys in the late 1990s as a player development consultant. Five players, including stars Michael Irvin and Leon Lett, had served league suspensions for drug violations. Owner Jerry Jones hired Hill to help players cope with their riches and the temptations that accompany wealth and fame.

Hill had proven his mentoring abilities with his own son, NBA star Grant Hill. "Calvin was uniquely qualified for the position," said Cowboys' public relations director Rich Dalrymple.

Three decades after the Cowboys drafted Hill, he was still contributing to the team.

60 Check out New Stadium

In 2009, the Cowboys will move from Texas Stadium to a new $1 billion stadium. If you want to attend any games, you'd better be rich. Fans will have to pay from $16,000 to $150,000 per seat just for the right to buy season tickets. The tickets themselves, $340 per game, are extra. Those prices are flooring a lot of folks. Previously, owner Jerry Jones had hinted that he might charge $10,000 for the right to buy tickets. The new stadium, which hasn't been named yet, will be the finest in the league. Would you expect anything less from Jones?

"He's breaking new ground here," said Robert Baade, a sports economist. "This is a risky business for the team, but Jerry Jones has proven to be a financial maverick."

The Cowboys' current home, Texas Stadium, opened in 1971 in the suburb of Irving. It's served the Cowboys well, and, with its unique hole in the roof is easily recognizable. However, Texas Stadium seats only 66,000, making it obsolete by today's standards.

The new stadium in nearby Arlington will normally seat 80,000 but can be expanded to 100,000. The stadium will have a huge retractable roof that can be closed in inclement weather. The Texas Stadium roof, by contrast, isn't retractable.

The spectacular new stadium will have four massive, signature arches rising 320 feet above the field to support the roof. Enormous retractable glass doors will open at either end zone. Above the field, several large video monitors will be clearly visible to everyone in the stadium. About 200 luxury suites will be spread throughout the stadium, including some at sideline level.

"The new Dallas Cowboys stadium stands as a monumental physical expression of the team: dominant and powerful in stature, simple and purposeful in nature," according to its architect, HKS Inc. of Dallas.

When the Cowboys moved from the Cotton Bowl to Texas Stadium, some fans griped because ticket prices skyrocketed. But at least fans could buy a single-game ticket. At the new stadium, the Cowboys hope to sell every seat as part of a season package.

In early 2008, team officials announced that early ticket sales were brisk for the new stadium. Dallas fans are among the most rabid in the league, and many have lots of money. It's probably a safe bet that all 80,000 seats will be sold before the first kickoff in 2009.

Exorbitant ticket prices may simply be a tradeoff for a championship-caliber team in today's NFL. After all, Jones just gave quarterback Tony Romo a $67 million contract. That money has to come from somewhere.

For those who can't afford tickets, we'll simply have to yell louder at home. Jones makes no apologies for setting ticket prices in the stratosphere. "There's no question the new stadium is going to continue to add energy to this team and be attractive to free agents who might come to this team," Jones said.

61 Visit Cotton Bowl

The Cotton Bowl, the Cowboys' first home, doesn't look so good these days. After all, it's almost 80 years old. The city of Dallas, which owns the venerable old stadium, has committed to spending millions to refurbish it for college games and other events.

Back in the 1960s, though, the 75,000-seat Cotton Bowl was a proud facility. Toward the end of the decade, when the Cowboys had become an elite team, they filled up the open-air stadium. Fans cheered as quarterback Don Meredith threw a bomb to Bullet Bob Hayes or defensive tackle Bob Lilly hurled a quarterback to the ground.

The Cotton Bowl was the site of the 1966 NFL Championship Game between the Cowboys and Green Bay Packers. The Cowboys, in only their seventh season, had the jitters early on and fell behind, 14–0. They came back, however, and scared the Packers before losing, 34–27.

The Cowboys moved from the Cotton Bowl to Texas Stadium in 1971. Since then, it's slipped further back in the pages of Cowboy history. That's a shame. Two generations of fans have no idea where the team got its start. When the new Cowboys stadium opens in 2009, the Cotton Bowl will recede even further from memory.

These days, people have few chances to watch a game at the Cotton Bowl.

The biggest event is the annual Texas-Oklahoma game in October. Each year, the Cotton Bowl sells out as red-clad OU fans drive south from Norman and orange-blooded Texas fans drive north from Austin. It's worth attending a Texas-OU game to get feel the excitement that was present when the Cowboys occupied the Cotton Bowl.

Over the years, Dallas officials have occasionally discussed tearing down the Cotton Bowl. Thankfully, preservationists always step in and stop the wrecking balls.

If you visit the Cotton Bowl—and Cowboy fans should—you may be shocked at the conditions. Don't expect to find a modern stadium with luxury boxes and wide concourses. The Cotton Bowl is a creaky old structure, dark and dank in places. Some of its concrete exterior is stained and chipping away. But, as with anyone's first home, the Cotton Bowl will always hold special memories for the Cowboys. It's a shame they don't play any preseason or exhibition games at the Cotton Bowl. They've severed all ties to the historic stadium.

Understandably, the Cowboys might want to forget their first few years at the Cotton Bowl. They were a dismal team. In their first season in 1960, the

Cowboys didn't win a game, finishing 0–11–1. The tie came on the road.

In 1962, Dallas won four games (two at the Cotton Bowl), and in 1963 they won five games (three at home). Fans were slow to embrace the Cowboys. The first home sellout didn't occur until 1965, when the Cowboys finished 7–7, their first .500 season. Today, it's hard to imagine the Cowboys not selling out even a few games in a season.

By the end of the 1960s, the Cowboys had become a hugely successful, high-profile team. They needed a glitzy new stadium. Owner Clint Murchison Jr. snubbed Dallas officials and built Texas Stadium in the adjacent suburb of Irving. Fortunately, the team wasn't renamed the Irving Cowboys.

The Cotton Bowl was left with the crumbs, hosting a few college and high school games each year, as it fell into disrepair. Even if you don't ever attend a game at the Cotton Bowl, you owe it to yourself to walk around the exterior. It's easily accessible off Interstate 30 near downtown Dallas. The Cotton Bowl is located on the state fairgrounds, and they're open year-round.

When you go, gaze up at the steep stadium walls. Close your eyes and imagine a Meredith bomb to Hayes for a touchdown. Hear the crowd roar its approval for the young, rapidly developing team. The Cowboys grew up and matured at the Cotton Bowl. It deserves some respect.

62 Clint Longley

Clint Longley had a short but eventful career. He pulled off a miraculous comeback victory as a rookie quarterback in 1974. But less than two years later, he was gone after he did the unthinkable and punched starting quarterback Roger Staubach, a Dallas hero.

The Cowboys traded Longley to San Diego, where he languished as a backup for a year before being cut. He never returned to the NFL. Talk about an abrupt ending to a promising career.

Let's start with his first big splash as a Cowboy. It occurred on November

28, 1974, in a game against the rival Washington Redskins. Longley, a rookie, hadn't played all year. He came into the game midway through the third quarter after Staubach suffered a concussion.

The Cowboys trailed the Redskins, 16–3. In his first drive, Longley moved the team downfield and hit tight end Billy Joe DuPree for a 35-yard touchdown. In the fourth quarter, Longley led another drive that ended with a 1-yard touchdown run. Remarkably, he had the Cowboys on top, 17–16.

But the Redskins' Duane Thomas, a former Cowboy, scored on a 19-yard run to put Washington back in the lead, 23–17. Only 45 seconds remained in the game, and Dallas had time for one last drive. Longley, unfazed by the pressure, moved the Cowboys to midfield with 35 seconds left. The Redskins brought in seven defensive backs to guard against a long touchdown pass.

No matter. Longley spotted a streaking Drew Pearson on the right sideline and threw a perfect strike. Pearson caught the ball at the 4-yard line and ran in for the score. Dallas won, 24–23. Teammates mobbed the rookie.

"A triumph of the uncluttered mind," offensive guard Blaine Nye pronounced in amazement.

Despite his magnificent performance, Longley returned to the bench the next week and played little in 1975. After the season, the Cowboys signed quarterback Danny White, who would be groomed as Staubach's replacement. Longley seemed threatened by White's arrival, and he didn't talk to White or Staubach during training camp in 1976.

Only days before the start of the season, Longley was throwing passes to Pearson in practice. Pearson dropped a pass, and Longley yelled at him. Staubach, standing nearby, took offense at this young kid rebuking his favorite receiver. Staubach and Longley started jawing and met after practice on a nearby field.

Longley threw a punch at Staubach, grazing his head. Staubach pounced on Longley and pinned him to the ground. Assistant coach Dan Reeves had to intervene and separate the two.

"If I were you, I'd be careful," Reeves warned Staubach. "I wouldn't turn my back on him."

Staubach should have heeded his advice. A few days later, Longley approached Staubach in the locker room as he was lacing up his shoulder pads. Without saying a word, Longley punched Staubach, knocking him into some equipment and opening a cut over his left eye.

Before Staubach could react, Longley bolted from the locker room, caught a ride to the airport and never returned to the team. Staubach has never spoken to him again. "I'd prefer to keep it that way, too," he wrote in his autobiography.

Longley became a vagabond after leaving the NFL. He played briefly for the Hamilton Tiger-Cats of the Canadian Football League and the Shreveport Steamer of the American Football Association. He then worked as a sportswriter for a weekly newspaper in the Dallas area. Finally, he moved to South Texas and lived near the beach.

He rarely talks about his run-in with Staubach.

"What happened between Roger and me is something I don't think about," Longley told a writer years ago. "That was a long time ago."

True, but the incident will never be forgotten.

63 Shotgun Offense and Flex Defense

Tom Landry used to think outside the box before anyone used that phrase. He enjoyed devising new offensive or defensive wrinkles that would give opposing teams headaches.

Landry operated like a mad scientist. He didn't mind going against convention if he thought an idea had promise. Two examples: the shotgun offense and flex defense.

Landry began using the shotgun in 1975, a year after the Cowboys missed the playoffs for the first time in nine years. He thought the anemic offense needed a boost. The shotgun, a formation in which the quarterback stands five yards behind center, is intended to give the quarterback more time to survey the field.

Landry didn't invent the shotgun, but he began using it on the suggestion of two assistant coaches. "It looked strange and drew some criticism at first," he said.

Quarterback Roger Staubach, however, liked the formation because it gave him another second or two to release the ball. "Going to the shotgun is such an obvious alternative," he said.

The new formation shotgun produced immediate results. The Cowboys won their first four games of the 1975 season and finished 10–4 to earn a wild-card playoff spot. One of their most famous plays came out of the shotgun.

The Cowboys trailed the heavily favored Minnesota Vikings, 14–10, with only 24 seconds left. With the ball at the 50-yard line, Staubach lined up in the shotgun and heaved a bomb to Drew Pearson. He outmaneuvered two defenders to catch the ball and score a touchdown. Dallas won, 17–14, and later advanced to Super Bowl X.

After the 1975 season, the shotgun became an integral part of Dallas' offense. Eventually, almost every NFL team began using it and most still do. Imitation is the sincerest form of flattery.

The flex defense, like the shotgun, became critical to the Cowboys' early success. Landry devised the system in the mid-1960s and kept it until he was fired in 1989. The flex defense uses four defensive linemen and three linebackers. The idea was that defenders didn't instinctively pursue the ball carrier. Instead, they guarded a spot on the field.

Many players had a hard time adjusting to the flex, because it required them to suppress their natural tendency to chase the football. Even some of the Cowboys' best players weren't sold on it.

"It's been said that by the time you truly understand the flex, you're too old to play," defensive end Harvey Martin said.

Lee Roy Jordan, an All-Pro middle linebacker, had a more positive view of the flex.

"It was a great concept," Jordan said. "Once you got it down, you could really make it work."

Unlike the shotgun, the flex didn't catch on with other teams. As Landry said, "It took a lot of character to play the flex."

In the latter days of his coaching career, Landry stuck with the flex despite criticism that it had outlived its usefulness. When Jimmy Johnson became coach, he immediately scrapped it.

Still, the flex worked for many years and helped the Doomsday Defense become dominant. Landry deserves credit for devising the flex and staying with it, even if his players grumbled.

64 Preston Pearson

In the NFL, one team's castoff can become another team's star. No one illustrates that more than Preston Pearson.

The Pittsburgh Steelers cut Pearson shortly before the 1975 season, and the Cowboys, desperate for a running back, picked him up. The previous year, Dallas' second-leading rusher, Robert Newhouse, gained only 501 yards. Even though Pearson was 30 years old, coach Tom Landry thought he could help.

He was right. Pearson started the final 10 games of the season, finishing with 509 yards rushing and 351 yards receiving.

"I thought he would be a very good fit on our team because of his ability to run draws and screens, and be a third-down or long-yardage back," said Gil Brandt, player personnel director. "He turned out to be an even better player than we thought he would be."

Pearson's biggest game came in the playoffs against the Los Angeles Rams. He caught seven passes for 123 yards and scored three touchdowns. The Cowboys routed the Rams, 37–7. "I was in the zone," Pearson said.

Pearson, a big back at 6' 2" and 210 pounds, had an uncanny knack for getting open. He didn't have blazing speed, but he could catch a short screen pass in the flat and zigzag his way past linebackers and defensive backs.

"He could run routes, read defenses, and make adjustments," Newhouse said. "He had abilities that no one else on our team had."

Pearson became a permanent fixture in passing situations. He essentially created the third-down specialist that has become such a big part of the game.

In 1976, Pearson had a disappointing season after suffering a knee injury. He missed several games and rushed for only 233 yards. In 1977, the running back of the future, No. 1 draft pick Tony Dorsett, arrived. Many people expected him to start immediately. But Landry wanted to ease him into the lineup.

He let Pearson start the first nine games until Dorsett took over. Pearson had a marvelous year, rushing for 341 yards and catching 46 passes, a team record for a running back. Dallas finished 12–2, swept through the playoffs, and beat Denver, 27–10, in Super Bowl XII. Pearson led the team with five catches.

Even with the development of Dorsett, Pearson continued to make major contributions. In 1978, for instance, he caught 47 passes for 526 yards. The Cowboys advanced to Super Bowl XIII to meet Pearson's old team, the Steelers. Pittsburgh won, 35–31.

The next two seasons, Pearson's receiving numbers tailed off, and he retired after the 1980 season. Pearson had a remarkable 14-year career, especially considering that he didn't play football in college. Instead, he starred in basketball at Illinois. The Baltimore Colts liked his athletic ability and drafted him in the 12th round in 1967. They tried him at defensive back before converting him to running back.

Pearson played for the Colts, mainly in a backup role, for three seasons. In 1970, the Colts traded Pearson to Pittsburgh. His playing time increased, but he never became a star. In 1971, his best year, Pearson rushed for 605 yards. In his last year, 1974, his rushing total dipped to 317 yards. The Steelers cut him, and the Cowboys came calling.

"The Steelers really messed up when they let Preston go," Dallas defensive end Harvey Martin said.

No one would disagree.

65 Tony Hill

When people think of the greatest Cowboy receiver of the 1970s, they usually think of Drew Pearson. No wonder. Roger Staubach and Pearson teamed up for countless big plays during the decade.

But Pearson's counterpart, Tony Hill, also had a great career. In fact, Hill was bigger, faster, and probably had more talent than Pearson. Pearson simply worked harder and squeezed more out of his abilities.

The Cowboys drafted Hill in the third round in 1977 out of Stanford. There, he set all the school's receiving records. As a rookie, Hill played only occasionally before winning a starting role his second season. He had a tremendous year, catching 46 passes for 823 yards and scoring six touchdowns. In 1979, Hill's third year, he did even better. He caught 60 passes for 1,062 yards and scored 10 touchdowns. He was named to the Pro Bowl and got the nickname Thrill Hill.

He and Pearson formed a potent one-two punch at receiver from 1978 until 1983, when Pearson retired. Statistically, Hill outshone Pearson. Every year during that period, Hill had more receptions and gained more yards. In every season but one, Hill scored more touchdowns.

Hill, like Pearson, made some dramatic catches. His most memorable occurred on December 16, 1979. Dallas trailed the rival Washington Redskins, 34–28, with 1:46 left in the game. The Cowboys started their last drive on their own 25-yard line. On first down, Staubach hit Hill for 20 yards.

He then connected with Pearson twice to give Dallas a first down on the Washington 8-yard line with just 45 seconds left. A first-down pass to Hill fell incomplete. On the next play, Staubach lofted a perfect ball to Hill, who made an over-the-shoulder catch for a touchdown. Dallas won, 35–34, knocking Washington out of playoff contention.

Hill had other outstanding games. In 1980, he caught a 28-yard

Tony Hill holds the ball high as he runs into end zone for a touchdown in Super Bowl XIII in Miami.

touchdown pass with 45 seconds left to give Dallas a 27–24 victory over St. Louis. In the 1983 season opener, he caught touchdowns of 75 and 51 yards to help Dallas overcome a 20–point deficit and beat Washington, 31–30. In a wild-card playoff game later that year, Hill set a Cowboys' playoff record with nine catches.

Hill, however, didn't achieve the recognition of Pearson. Pearson had the benefit of playing with Staubach for more seasons. Staubach was well known for directing come-from-behind victories, and Pearson was on the receiving end of many late scores. The most famous was Pearson's Hail Mary catch against the Minnesota Vikings in a 1975 playoff game. Staubach heaved a 50-yard touchdown pass to Pearson with 24 seconds left to give Dallas a 17–14 victory.

Pearson made more clutch catches than Hill, particularly across the middle. Hill, on the other hand, preferred to catch balls near the sidelines and use his speed to break a long gain.

"Tony's our big-play guy," coach Tom Landry once said. "He threatens the defense because he has the excellent burst of speed to get under a ball that's deep. He's a very explosive player, the type that can turn a short play into a deep play in a hurry."

After Pearson retired in 1983, Hill became the focus of the passing game. In 1984, he missed five games with a shoulder injury, but still caught 58 passes and led the team in receiving yards for the seventh straight year. In 1985, Hill had his best season. He caught 74 passes for more than 1,000 yards and scored seven touchdowns. In 1986, his last year with the Cowboys, his receptions dropped to 49.

Even though fans don't immediately recall Hill, he had an outstanding 10-year career. He caught 479 passes, third-most in team history, and gained 7,988 yards, second-most in team history. Hill made the Pro Bowl three times and had one stretch in which he caught a pass in 72 straight games.

Not bad for a guy who played in Drew Pearson's shadow.

Click on dallascowboys.com

Every NFL team has a website. So what's special about dallascowboys.com? It's one of the most thorough, easy-to-navigate, interesting sites in the league. The writers, who work for owner Jerry Jones, are even allowed to be critical of the team. The stories offer good insight, and don't read like news releases.

If the Cowboys stink one game, the writers can say so. Some NFL websites seem to have a good-news-only edict. By contrast, the lead writer for dallascowboys.com is Mickey Spagnola, a highly respected, former Dallas newspaper reporter who doesn't pull any punches.

After the Cowboys lost to the Washington Redskins in the last game of the 2007 season, he said the Redskins "thoroughly outplayed" the "sluggish" Cowboys. True.

Besides an honest assessment of the Cowboys, the website has an excellent year-by-year history of the team. It starts in 1960, the Cowboys' first year, and continues to the present. You can click on any year and get a brief overview of the season, such as win-loss record, starting lineups, and Pro Bowl selections. For stats freaks, the site gives detailed year-end offensive and defensive numbers for the Cowboys and their opponents.

Let's illustrate what you can find. In 1986, for example, the Cowboys played a preseason game in London, recorded their 100th win at Texas Stadium, and had their first losing season in 20 years.

Now let's look at 1992. The Cowboys won the first of three Super Bowls in the 1990s, Emmitt Smith won his second league rushing title, and the Cowboys set a team record with 13 regular-season wins.

In recent years, the website has added a multimedia link. You can view game highlights and clips from post-game press conferences and player interviews.

The section also has photos of games, training camp, and the Dallas Cowboys Cheerleaders. Check out the latter. If you're infatuated with the cheerleaders, you can order a host of merchandise, including photos, calendars, T-shirts, a tote bag, Christmas tree ornament, and a Dallas Cowboys Cheerleaders Barbie® doll.

Dallasnews.com also offers a preview of the team's new $1 billion stadium that will open in 2009. It will seat up to 100,000 fans and have a massive retractable roof. The Cowboys have already landed Super Bowl XLV to be played there in 2011.

The obvious question, will the Cowboys be one of the teams?

67 Rayfield Wright

Rayfield Wright took an unlikely path to the Hall of Fame. For starters, he played college football at tiny Fort Valley State. One of his positions was safety.

Once he became a Cowboy, Wright morphed into a 6' 6", 260-pound offensive lineman who dominated opponents. He also played a little tight end and defensive end on his way to Canton.

The Cowboys chose Wright in the seventh round of the 1967 draft. He settled at right tackle, and, in 1971, began a string of six straight Pro Bowl appearances. He earned the nickname Big Cat because of his quickness.

Wright never lacked confidence. In 1969, he was scheduled to face legendary defensive lineman Deacon Jones of the Los Angeles Rams. Before the game, a teammate told Wright he might have a long afternoon.

"Why?" Wright asked.

"Because Deacon is big, and he's fast," his teammate replied.

"Well, I'm big and fast," Wright answered.

He backed up his words with a big game, neutralizing Jones [Note: Cowboys played the Rams in 1969 preseason, but not during regular season].

"I never worried about football after that game," Wright said. "I knew I could play."

He was part of a stellar offensive line that also featured Pro Bowlers Ralph Neely and John Niland. Wright played in five Super Bowls during his 12-year career. In 1977, Wright suffered a serious knee injury that he battled until he retired in 1979.

During his 13-year career, Wright protected Roger Staubach and opened holes for a pair of 1,000-yard rushers, Calvin Hill and Tony Dorsett. All the while, Wright remained a kind, soft-spoken gentleman—never a player who taunted his opponents. "He was the very best at his position in the NFL," Staubach said.

Excerpts from Wright's
Hall of Fame Acceptance Speech

"I learned a poem in the eighth grade entitled, "The Road Not Taken." It's about two roads. One was well traveled. The other was grassy and wanted wear. Through the poem, I discovered that life would give me choices. It was recognizing those choices that proved to be the greatest challenge …

"Success didn't come my way instantly. In fact, I went out for football in high school, and I couldn't make the team in my first three years …

"I've had many mentors in my life who always said, 'Let honor and success come to you only if it's deserved, not because it's sought after' …

"I wish to tip my hat to the Dallas Cowboys fans, especially the ones who remember my playing days and America's Team of the '70s …

"Now, parents, teach your children well. Encourage them with your faith and leadership. Remember that you are the windows through which your children see this world …

"To every young athlete within the sound of my voice, it takes courage to dream your dream. Don't let them sit in the locker room. Take a leap of faith. Listen to your parents and respect your elders. Learn from your successes and your losses …

"Be satisfied you gave the game everything you had and remember this: Don't be afraid to travel the road less traveled because Larry Rayfield Wright did, and you can, too."

Many teammates and opposing players thought Wright should have been inducted into the Hall of Fame as soon as he became eligible, five years after his retirement. Instead, he had to wait 27 years until his induction in 2006.

"Justice has been done," Dorsett said upon his induction. "Talk to anyone in the Pro Football Hall of Fame from Deacon Jones on down, and they all say a player of Rayfield Wright's caliber is more than deserving of being in the Hall of Fame."

Early in his career, Wright remained patient as coaches tried him at different positions.

"He was always a team player whose solid character contributed to a winning atmosphere," coach Tom Landry said. "It was an honor to coach Rayfield Wright."

68 Dirty Dozen

The Cowboys had modest expectations for the 1975 season. They had just come off an 8–6 year in which they missed the playoffs for the first time in nine years. Pro Bowl defensive tackle Bob Lilly, a future Hall of Famer, had retired. Running back Calvin Hill, another Pro Bowler, had defected to the upstart World Football League.

But the Cowboys surprised the league by going 10–4 and earning a wild-card playoff berth. They wound up in Super Bowl X, narrowly losing to the Pittsburgh Steelers, 21–17. The Dirty Dozen helped account for the Cowboys' unlikely success. The name refers to 11 rookies and one free agent who made the 1975 team. Nine eventually became starters, and five made the Pro Bowl.

The draft class is one of the best in NFL history and laid a solid foundation for the Cowboys' future. The Dirty Dozen included Randy White, Bob Breunig, and Thomas Hollywood Henderson.

"Our youth seemed to add a spark of life to the veteran players," Breunig said. "At midseason, we all grew beards, so we were dubbed the Dirty Dozen."

The players would propel Dallas to three Super Bowl appearances over the next four seasons. White undoubtedly had the best career of the Dirty Dozen. He struggled his first two seasons as coaches tried him at linebacker. But after they moved him to defensive tackle, he flourished. He punished opposing quarterbacks and running backs for the next 13 years. He was named co-Most Valuable Player (along with defensive end Harvey Martin) in Super Bowl XII.

Henderson had a brief but spectacular career. He was one of the most gifted athletes in Cowboys' history. Even though he was a linebacker, he could outrun most backs and receivers. "He was so athletic, strong, and bright that pro football came easy to him," defensive back Charlie Waters said.

Unfortunately, Henderson didn't handle success well. As he acknowledged in his autobiography, he began using drugs early in his career, even snorting cocaine on the sidelines during Super Bowl XIII. His play became erratic and his behavior unpredictable. He missed team meetings and practices. Coach Tom Landry tried to be patient with Henderson because of his enormous talent, but finally he had enough and cut Henderson late in the 1979 season.

The Dirty Dozen also included Randy Hughes, an All-American safety from Oklahoma who seemed destined for the Pro Bowl. He backed up Cliff Harris and Charlie Waters his first four years, then earned a starting role in 1979. But a series of shoulder separations ended his career in 1981. He'll be remembered for an outstanding performance in Super Bowl XII. He intercepted a pass and recovered two fumbles.

Other members of the Dirty Dozen who had relatively undistinguished careers were running back Scott Laidlaw, center Kyle Davis, defensive back Rolly Woolsey, and punter Mitch Hoopes.

The one free agent in the Dirty Dozen was Percy Howard, a wide receiver. He played only one season before a knee injury ended his career. But he had a moment in the spotlight: a 34-yard touchdown reception in Super Bowl X. It turned out to be the only catch of his brief career, giving him a unique place in Cowboys' history.

In the 30-plus drafts since 1975, the Cowboys have never hit the jackpot like they did with the Dirty Dozen, and they probably never will.

69 Draft Duds

Drafting players is part science, part luck. Sometimes a can't-miss player winds up being a colossal bust. The Cowboys have had their share of white elephants. In fact, a string of top-round draft duds doomed the Cowboys to their steep decline in the mid-1980s.

Here are the top 10 draft busts in Cowboys' history. The list includes the year they were selected and their position. All, except for Jesse Penn—a second-round selection—were No. 1 picks.

(1). Rod Hill, 1982, defensive back. The Cowboys have found many outstanding players at small colleges. They thought Hill, who played at Kentucky State, would be another, but he wasn't. He lasted only two years and shouldn't have been around that long. He didn't produce, and he had poor work habits. He once told teammates he was a "fanatic about college basketball." Veteran safety Dennis Thurman replied, "I wish you were a fanatic about learning to play cornerback in the NFL." Hill made one of his biggest blunders in the 1982 NFC Championship Game against the Washington Redskins. He fumbled a punt deep in Dallas territory, and the Redskins recovered. They quickly scored a touchdown to increase their lead to 14–3 en route to a 31–17 win.

(2). Shante Carver, 1994, defensive end. The Cowboys handed Carver a starting role because of retirements and injuries, but he did nothing to hold on to it. After four years, the Cowboys sent him packing. The Cowboys desperately needed a defensive end in 1994, and they didn't accurately assess Carver. "We let ourselves get talked into taking a defensive end no matter what," scouting director Larry Lacewell said.

(3). Bill Thomas, 1972, running back. Although he had size and speed, Thomas just couldn't play football. In his rookie training camp, he suffered a shoulder injury and missed half the season. When he returned, he didn't have a single carry. His total contributions consisted of two kickoff returns. Before the 1973 season, he was traded to Houston.

(4). David LaFleur, 1997, tight end. He was a huge 6' 7" and 272 pounds, fast, and had good hands. Plus, he had starred at a football powerhouse, LSU. LaFleur seemed like the ultimate can't-miss pick. Before the draft, the Cowboys sent quarterback Troy Aikman to practice with him, and Aikman delivered a glowing report. LaFleur played for four years and was an off-

and-on starter, but he never had a consistent impact. His best year was 1999, when he started every game and caught seven touchdown passes. But the next year, he caught only 12 passes and scored just one touchdown. The Cowboys cut him.

(5). Danny Noonan, 1987, defensive tackle. The Cowboys envisioned Noonan as the next Randy White. Like White, Noonan practically lived in the weight room. Like White, Noonan was an All-American in college, but he simply never made plays. A variety of injuries kept him out of the lineup for long stretches. In 1992, the Cowboys traded Noonan to the Green Bay Packers, who promptly cut him after six games. He never played again.

(6). Kevin Brooks, 1985, defensive tackle. Brooks was an awesome specimen at 6' 6" and 273 pounds, but he was a classic underachiever. His demise couldn't be blamed on injuries, either. Brooks managed to last four years, starting most games in 1987 and 1988. He never played like a No. 1 draft pick. The Cowboys traded him to Detroit after the 1988 season.

(7). Howard Richards, 1981, offensive lineman. The Cowboys expected Richards to immediately bolster the line and have a long, productive career, but he didn't. He played six years, never starting more than eight games in a season. Injuries hampered him, beginning with a groin injury in 1983 and continuing with a season-ending knee injury in 1984. Richards never fully recovered from knee surgery and was cut after the 1986 season.

(8). Billy Cannon Jr., 1984, linebacker. He starred at Texas A&M, and fans were excited about seeing a native son as the top draft choice. He probably had the shortest career of any No. 1 pick ever. In the eighth game of his rookie year, Cannon injured his neck. Doctors advised him to retire to avoid the possibility of more serious damage.

(9). Mike Sherrard, 1986, receiver. The Cowboys needed a big-play receiver to take the place of Pro Bowlers Drew Pearson and Tony Hill, who had recently retired. Sherrard, a No. 1 pick from UCLA, seemed like the guy. As a rookie, he caught 41 passes, scored five touchdowns, and led the team with an average of 18.1 yards per catch. But during the 1987 training camp, Sherrard suffered a compound fracture of both bones in his right leg and he missed the season. Before the 1988 season, he re-fractured his leg and missed another entire year. In 1989, the Cowboys released him.

(10). Jesse Penn, 1985, linebacker. The Cowboys thought they had a steal when they drafted Penn in the second round. At Virginia Tech, he had been an outstanding defensive end. Coaches thought they could convert him into a big-play linebacker. He had great size (6' 3" and 218 pounds) and speed. He showed promise early. In the preseason of his rookie year, he returned an interception 77 yards for a touchdown. During the regular season, he ran back a blocked punt 46 yards for a touchdown. But he never successfully fully made the transition to linebacker. His inconsistent play frustrated coaches, and he was cut after his second season in 1986.

70 Don Perkins

Don Perkins is the Cowboys' forgotten running back. He had a solid eight-year career, although he never put up the gaudy rushing numbers of those who followed him, such as Calvin Hall or Tony Dorsett. Perkins is important because he was the Cowboys' first star running back.

He played from 1961, the Cowboys' second year, until 1968. He never rushed for 1,000 yards. His highest total was 945 yards, but he made the Pro Bowl six times in recognition of his durability and consistency. Along with quarterback Don Meredith, Perkins endured the dismal seasons of the franchise.

Perkins had been an all-conference running back at New Mexico for three years, and the Cowboys had high expectations. He immediately disappointed

Don Perkins plunges through right tackle for a touchdown in a December 1967 game against the Cleveland Browns.

coaches by reporting to his first training camp 20 pounds overweight. He blamed his biscuit and gravy training diet. Perkins couldn't even complete the Landry Mile, a mandatory run up a nearby mountain.

"He looked absolutely awful," general manager Tex Schramm said. "We didn't know what to think."

Later, he broke his foot and didn't play his entire rookie year. The next year, he reported to camp in fine shape and had an outstanding season. Perkins, 5' 10" and 200 pounds, had 815 yards rushing and 298 yards receiving. "Perkins turned out to be the biggest highlight of the year," Landry said.

Perkins was an outstanding blocker known for his toughness. He once played an entire quarter with a broken arm. He had one of his best games in the 1966 NFL Championship against the Green Bay Packers. He rushed for 108 yards as the Cowboys fell, 34–27.

Perkins was only 31 when he retired. Actually, he had discussed retiring two years earlier. He told Schramm in 1966 that he wanted to quit to spend more time with his wife and four children, but Schramm talked him out of it.

Perkins then had two solid years, rushing for 823 yards in 1967 and 836 yards in 1968.

"Looking back, I'm pleased to say those last two years were among my most productive," he said.

The Cowboys inducted Perkins into the Ring of Honor in 1976. Perkins said he was always grateful Landry didn't cut him after he failed to complete the Landry Mile.

"Without his patience and fairness, nothing I eventually accomplished would have been possible," Perkins said. "He gave me a break, and in return, I gave him my best shot."

71 Walt Garrison

Walt Garrison had a nine-year career as a Cowboy, but his career as a cowboy continued long after his playing days.

Garrison was the kind of cowboy who competed in rodeos. He did so before he became a professional football player, and afterward, too. He rode bulls, wrestled steers, and roped calves. Running with a football seems easy compared to those pursuits.

Garrison was a rough-and-tumble fullback, as hard to bring down as an angry steer. He never had much speed. Garrison didn't make his yardage down the sidelines. He gained tough yardage up the middle with tacklers draped all over him. Former Dallas Cowboys quarterback Don Meredith liked to make a joke about Garrison's speed.

"If you needed four yards, you could give the ball to Walt, and he'd get you four yards," Meredith said. "If you needed 20 yards, you could give the ball to Walt, and he'd get you four yards."

During his career from 1966 to 1974, Garrison averaged 4.3 yards per carry. Garrison, who was 6' and 210 pounds, became a starter after Don Perkins retired in 1968.

He played alongside two speedy, elusive running backs, Calvin Hill and Duane Thomas. Garrison always performed well in big games. In Super Bowl VI, for instance, he gained 74 yards as the Cowboys knocked off the Miami Dolphins, 24–3. The year before, he demonstrated his toughness by playing with a cracked ankle in the 1970 NFC Championship Game. He ran for 71 yards as Dallas won, 17–10.

"Any other back would have stayed out for the rest of the day," coach Tom Landry said. "I remember going over to Walt and asking if he thought he could go. He said yes, that he was going to be okay. Actually, it was obvious that he was just about to die. But he was that determined to play."

Landry always valued Garrison, despite his lack of speed. During one training camp, Landry told Garrison not to run a 40-yard dash with the other veterans. Garrison asked why. He recounts the incident in his autobiography, *Once a Cowboy*.

"Walt," he said, and he's sort of whispering to me with his arm around my shoulder, "look, if those rookies ever find out how slow you are and you've been playing for six years, they'll think it's a snap to make this team."

Besides running like a bull, Garrison was an effective receiver. In 1971, he led the Cowboys with 40 receptions. During his career, he caught 182 passes and scored nine receiving touchdowns.

When the Cowboys signed Garrison as a fifth-round draft pick out of Oklahoma State, they offered him a new Pontiac Grand Prix as a bonus. He turned it down. Instead, he asked for a new horse trailer, and got it.

Ironically, he was driven from football by an injury he suffered in rodeo. After the 1974 season, he tore up a knee while wrestling a bull in Montana.

"I didn't plan to retire, and I probably would have played another year, maybe two, if I had not had to have a knee operation," Garrison wrote. "I hyper-extended it and tore all the ligaments and stuff."

After leaving football, Garrison appeared in TV commercials for years for smokeless tobacco. "Just a pinch between your cheek and gum for that full tobacco pleasure," he would say.

Garrison gained more recognition as a football player, but he enjoyed being a real cowboy more.

"If I could make as much money, I'd choose rodeoing over football," he once said. "To my way of thinking, it is the most demanding sport in the world."

72 Darren Woodson

Darren Woodson played linebacker in college, and he never lost his linebacker mentality, even after the Cowboys converted him to strong safety. Woodson loved to hit people.

Woodson, who was 6' 1" and 219 pounds, could cover the pass. He had plenty of interceptions and knocked-down passes. But he lived for making tackles, often at or near the line of scrimmage. In 2002, he became the Cowboys' all-time leader in tackles with 1,243. He broke a 26-year-old record held by middle linebacker Lee Roy Jordan. By the time Woodson retired in 2004, he had recorded 1,350 tackles.

Dallas drafted Woodson in the second round in 1992 out of Arizona State. When he joined the Cowboys, they were rapidly improving. Jimmy Johnson had just completed his third year as coach, and the Cowboys had improved from 1–15 to 11–5. As a rookie, Woodson started two games and played on special teams in the Cowboys' 52–17 drubbing of Buffalo in Super Bowl XXVII.

In his second year, Woodson became a starter. By his third year, 1994, Woodson made his first Pro Bowl team. He had five interceptions, returning one 94 yards for a touchdown. That same year, he suffered his first back

Darren Woodson smacks Oakland Raiders receiver Marcus Knight in an August 2003 game.

injury. A bad back would eventually force him to retire.

Woodson had hurt his back shortly before the biggest game of the season: the NFC Championship Game against the San Francisco 49ers. Woodson tried a variety of methods to ease the pain, but none worked. Finally, he resorted to a pain-killing shot only minutes before kickoff.

"You talk about some pain," Woodson said. "That area was tender, and he had to move the needle around for about 30 seconds to find the nerve, so he can numb it."

He was able to play, but he still wasn't 100 percent. Everyone expected a close game between Dallas and San Francisco, but the 49ers jumped out to an early 21–0 lead. Dallas committed three turnovers, an interception, and two fumbles, to essentially hand San Francisco the game. The Cowboys fought back but lost, 38–28.

"That was our best team, and we didn't even make it to the Super Bowl," Woodson said. "I don't care how good you are, you can't give a team like San Francisco 21 points in the first quarter and expect to come back and win."

For the next few years, his back didn't bother him. Before the 2004 season, he hurt it again while lifting weights. He didn't think it was serious, but the pain wouldn't go away. He eventually had surgery and hoped to return early in the year, but he never did. The back simply didn't improve enough to let him play.

A week before the end of the 2004 regular season, he announced his retirement after 13 years. Woodson finished his career with 23 interceptions. He was the last active member of the three Super Bowl championships of the '90s.

"It's hard to make a decision to not play because I've been playing since I was 8 years old," Woodson said in retiring. "It's a huge part of my life, but one thing football has never done is define me. My family is what defines me."

73 Roy Williams

Roy Williams quickly made a reputation in the NFL as a hard-hitting safety. He's still making headlines, but the news isn't always positive. Williams has been disciplined by the league four times in the past two seasons for horse-collar tackles. Those are tackles in which a defender grabs a player from behind around the collar and yanks him the ground.

Horse-collar tackles have been illegal since 2005, because they're dangerous. The player being tackled can easily hurt his legs as he's thrown backward. His cleats can get stuck in the turf, and his legs twist in odd directions. Terrell Owens, before joining the Cowboys, tore two ankle ligaments and suffered a broken leg when Williams horse-collared him in 2004.

In fact, that play helped persuade NFL officials to ban the tackles. Williams is having trouble avoiding them. In 2007, he was fined twice—$12,500 for his first illegal tackle in September, and $15,000 for another in October. When Williams made a third horse-collar tackle in December, the NFL suspended him without pay for one game.

Players know the danger of horse-collar tackles. Even Williams's teammates and coaches didn't rush to his defense when he was suspended. "That's the rule, and we need to abide by it," head coach Wade Phillips said. "He's just going to have to learn to do it different."

Williams' illegal tackles have hurt his reputation around the league. After the 2007 season, *The Sporting News* polled 107 players to find out the dirtiest player in the league. Williams came in third.

Despite his recent difficulties, Williams has had a fine career. He was the Cowboys' No. 1 draft pick in 2002 out of Oklahoma. In his final year, he earned All-American honors and was named Big 12 Defensive Player of the Year. In addition, he won the Jim Thorpe Award as the nation's outstanding defensive back and the Bronko Nagurski Award as the top defender.

As a rookie for the Cowboys, Williams immediately became a starter. He intercepted five passes, and returned two for touchdowns. In 2003, his second season, Williams made the Pro Bowl and has been chosen every year since.

Bill Parcells, who became Cowboys' coach in 2003, used to joke about Williams's size. He said Williams, at 6' and 225 pounds, is "a biscuit shy of being a linebacker." Williams, undoubtedly, is heavier and slower than many safeties. He has trouble covering speedy receivers, but he still makes big plays.

In every season, he's had at least two interceptions. In 2006, he had five. After the season, owner Jerry Jones signed Williams to a five-year, $25.2 million contract extension. It included an $11.1 million signing bonus, the highest ever for a safety. Williams was entering the final year of his contract and could have become an unrestricted free agent without a new deal.

"I am a Cowboy for life," Williams said.

Williams' teammates applauded the long-term deal. Owens said Williams intimidates opposing teams.

"He's one of those guys you have to be aware of on every given play," Owens said. "He'll bring it in the run game. He'll bring it in the passing game. He's like a double threat."

74 Attend Training Camp

Casual fans watch the Cowboys on television. Serious fans attend games, but hard-core fans attend training camp, and you should, too. You'll gain a greater appreciation for the intense preparation that goes into each season.

Every training camp has drama and suspense. Top draft choices arrive for their first camp, along with hopeful free agents. Every player is nervous, whether he shows it or not. It's intriguing to watch coaches survey the talent and make critical roster decisions.

During the Cowboys' long history, they've had numerous training camp locations. From 1963 to 1989, they held camp in Thousand Oaks, California, about 45 miles north of Los Angeles. The setting was beautiful, and the weather cool and predictable.

When Jerry Jones bought the team in 1989, he made wholesale changes, including moving training camp. He and new coach Jimmy Johnson wanted players to prepare for the season in a hotter environment in hopes of improving conditioning and toughness. In the Jones era, the Cowboys have held training camp in three Texas cities: Austin, San Antonio, and Wichita Falls.

For a fan, the location doesn't really matter. The nightlife in Austin is better than in Wichita Falls, but if you're truly coming to observe camp, not party at night, the drills and scrimmages look the same regardless of the setting.

Training camp always opens in late July and lasts about two weeks, ending just before the first exhibition game in early August. All practices are free and open to the public. The Cowboys' website, www.dallascowboys.com, lists the times. In 2007, for example, practices were held from 2:30 to 4:30 p.m. on most days. However, six "two-a-days" were scheduled. On those days, practices were held from 9 to 11 a.m. and from 3:30 to 5 p.m.

The Cowboys always inject entertainment into training camp. Jones wants to encourage fans to come and get excited about the upcoming season. In 2007, camp began with a "Kick-off Spectacular," a four-hour event inside the San Antonio Alamodome. It started with a concert by a rock band, then Jones, head coach Wade Phillips, and the players made appearances.

"How 'bout them Cowboys!" quarterback Tony Romo screamed to thousands of fans.

The Cowboys' website offers travel packages to attend training camp. For instance, you can get discounted tickets to San Antonio attractions such as SeaWorld and Six Flags. Jones, a marketing genius, has successfully promoted training camp as a can't-miss event for the true fan. People from throughout Texas and the nation attend. Patient fans can get autographs from most of the players.

Every camp brings a few surprises and special guests. In 2007, former Dallas cornerback Deion Sanders dropped by. He said he liked what he saw, even the inevitable skirmishes among players.

"I love to see fights break out," Sanders said. "That's a good sign. When nobody's fighting, there's something wrong with the climate."

Last year's camp also brought a daily Terrell Owens watch. Was the outspoken receiver happy? Was he hurt? Was he dropping passes or making big plans?

"Owens Sits out with Tired Legs," one news release read.

See what you're missing? Make it a point to attend training camp, especially now that the Cowboys have rejoined the NFL's elite.

75 Twenty Straight Winning Seasons

Great sports franchises win consistently. By that measure, the Cowboys are a great sports franchise. During one stretch in particular they had a remarkable run. From the mid-1960s to the mid-1980s, the Dallas Cowboys strung together 20 consecutive winning seasons. No other team has matched that feat before or since.

In the age of parity, the accomplishment may never be matched.

Back in the early 1960s, the Cowboys seemed like an unlikely candidate to compile a prolonged winning streak. In their first season in 1960, the Cowboys didn't win a game. In 1961, they won only four. They won five in 1962.

The winning seasons didn't begin until 1966 with a 10–3–1 mark. Then the Cowboys made winning seasons the norm. During the streak of 20 consecutive winning seasons, the Cowboys played in two NFL Championship Games and five Super Bowls.

In 1974, the Cowboys finished 8–6, almost snapping the streak. But they rebounded strong. They were 10–4 in 1975 and made it to Super Bowl X. The Cowboys lost, 21–17, to the Pittsburgh Steelers.

The Cowboys' best record during the 20-year period was in 1977. They finished 12–2 and, not surprisingly, won Super Bowl XII. The Cowboys downed the Denver Broncos, 27–10.

The streak could have been jeopardized in 1980, the first season following the retirement of quarterback Roger Staubach, the team's leader throughout the 1970s. But Danny White, who backed up Staubach for four years, stepped in as starter and kept the winning streak alive. He led the Cowboys to records of 12–4 in 1980, 12–4 in 1981, and 6–3 in strike-shortened 1982.

Each year, the Cowboys fell one game short of the Super Bowl, losing in the NFC Championship Game.

Remarkable Run

The Cowboys enjoyed 20 straight winning seasons from 1966 to 1985. Following are their regular-season records each year.

1966: 10–3–1
1967: 9–5
1968: 12–2
1969: 11–2–1
1970: 10–4 (lost Super Bowl V, 16–13, to Baltimore)
1971: 11–3 (won Super Bowl VI, 24–3, over Miami)
1972: 10–4
1973: 10–4
1974: 8–6
1975: 10–4 (lost Super Bowl X, 21–17, to Pittsburgh)
1976: 11–3
1977: 12–2 (won Super Bowl XII, 27–10, over Denver)
1978: 12–4 (lost Super Bowl XIII, 35–31, to Pittsburgh)
1979: 11–5
1980: 12–4
1981: 12–4
1982: 6–3 (strike-shortened season)
1983: 12–4
1984: 9–7
1985: 10–6

In 1984, the Cowboys compiled a shaky 9–7 record that included several narrow victories and the distraction of a quarterback controversy. Coach Tom Landry surprised many people by benching White and elevating his backup, Gary Hogeboom.

The next year, the Cowboys rebounded to 10–6. The streak of winning seasons finally ended in 1986. The Cowboys played well in the first half of the season, winning six of eight. They collapsed in the second half, winning only one game to finish 7–9.

The Cowboys then started the wrong kind of streak. From 1987 to 1990, they had a losing record each season, but happy times were just around the corner. In 1991, the Jimmy Johnson-led Cowboys improved to 11–5. In 1992, they finished 13–3 en route to a smashing victory in Super Bowl XXVII.

Despite winning three Super Bowls in four years, the Cowboys have never again put together even 10 straight winning seasons. All the more reasons to salute the Dallas Cowboy teams from 1966 to 1985.

76 1972 Comeback Against 49ers

Roger Staubach built his career on late, come-from-behind victories. He led the Cowboys to 23 wins after they trailed in the fourth quarter. Staubach's first dramatic comeback victory occurred in a wild-card playoff game against the San Francisco 49ers on December 23, 1972.

He wasn't even expected to play. Staubach had missed most of the season because of a shoulder separation he suffered in preseason. Craig Morton, whom Staubach had beat out in 1971, led the Cowboys during the 1972 regular season and into the playoffs. But he struggled against the 49ers, and the Cowboys trailed 28–13 near the end of the third quarter.

Coach Tom Landry decided to see if Staubach could ignite the team. At first, Staubach looked rusty. He was sacked, threw an incompletion, and lost a fumble. Still, Landry stuck with him. In the fourth quarter, the Cowboys made a short field goal to make the score 28–16. The 49ers' lead still seemed secure with only two minutes left in the game.

Then Staubach caught fire. He threw a 20-yard touchdown pass to Billy Parks to close the gap to 28–23 with 1:30 remaining. Dallas then recovered an onside kick. On first down, Staubach ran for 21 yards. Next, he hit Parks for 19 yards, moving the Cowboys to the San Francisco 10-yard line. On the ensuing play, Staubach avoided a heavy rush and found receiver Ron Sellers in the end zone. The touchdown gave the Cowboys an improbable 30–28 victory.

On the sidelines, the team erupted in celebration. Even the normally stoic Landry seemed beside himself.

"It was one of the most remarkable endings to a football game I'd ever seen," Landry wrote in his autobiography.

Staubach said the 49ers never shut the door on the Cowboys. "They kept goofing around, and we kept getting the ball back," he said. "All of a sudden, we scored 17 points. We made believers out of everyone."

Indeed. Staubach would make believers out of people his entire career.

"I was never in a situation where I thought we were going to lose or quit," he said. "We got beat, and we did lose, but we never quit. If you have that confidence, you get your share of comebacks."

General manager Tex Schramm said Staubach had intangible qualities that set him apart from Morton.

"Something bad always seemed to happen to Craig and something good to Roger," Schramm said. "And it wasn't necessarily their making. Maybe it was their attitude, the way they thought. Frankly, I don't know. There has to be some reason that, when two players both have good ability, one wins and the other loses."

77 Denied Three-peat

The Cowboys desperately wanted to win a third straight Super Bowl in 1994. No team had ever pulled off the feat. If the Cowboys could do so, they would be considered the greatest NFL team of all time.

A "three-peat" certainly seemed within their grasp. The Cowboys had rolled to two straight titles, demolishing Buffalo, 52–17, in Super Bowl XXVII, following up with a 30–13 drubbing of the Bills in Super Bowl XXVIII.

In 1994, the Cowboys still had the Triplets—the potent offensive trio of quarterback Troy Aikman, running back Emmitt Smith, and receiver Michael Irvin. The defense remained stout. The biggest question mark was new head coach Barry Switzer. He came aboard after owner Jerry

Jones fired Jimmy Johnson, the miracle-worker who transformed the Cowboys from a 1–15 laughingstock to a two-time Super Bowl champ in five years.

Under Switzer, the Cowboys got off to a strong start. They beat Pittsburgh, 26–9, in the opener, and Smith rushed for 171 yards. The Cowboys won eight of their first nine, and finished 12–4 to win their third-straight NFC East title. In the first round of the playoffs, the Cowboys steamrolled Green Bay, 35–9.

Now they would meet the 49ers in the NFC Championship Game. The winner would go to Super Bowl XXIX. The Cowboys had already beaten the 49ers in the 1992 and 1993 NFC Championship games and felt confident.

"We had San Francisco's number, and they weren't going to beat us," safety Darren Woodson said.

The 49ers had spent the off-season gearing up for another showdown with the Cowboys. They made the biggest free-agent signing in the league, inking Pro Bowl cornerback Deion Sanders. "I gave the 49ers a swagger they didn't have," he said.

No one could have imagined how the game would start. On Dallas' third play, Aikman threw a short pass that was intercepted and returned 44 yards for a touchdown. On the next drive, Irvin fumbled as he stretched for a first down. San Francisco quarterback Steve Young quickly hit running back Ricky Watters on a 29-yard touchdown pass to widen the 49ers' lead to 14–0. Only 4:19 had elapsed.

Disaster then struck for a third time. On the ensuing kickoff, Kevin Williams fumbled, and the 49ers recovered. Seven plays later, they scored on a one-yard run. At the midpoint of the first quarter, the 49ers held a commanding 21–0 lead.

"It was like a horror movie," Switzer said. "I couldn't believe it."

A three-touchdown deficit is hard to overcome against a weak team. Against a championship-caliber team like the 49ers, it's virtually insurmountable. "Never in a million years could I anticipate that we'd get into that kind of hole to start the game," Aikman said.

Switzer gathered his stunned players together.

"I turned to them and said, 'Guys, you know what's great about being down 21–0 after seven minutes,'" Switzer recalled. "They all looked at me like I'm crazy. I said, 'Because we got 53 minutes to get back in this SOB.'"

Dallas did. Late in the first quarter, Aikman threw a 44-yard touchdown pass to Irvin. In the second quarter, Smith scored on a 4-yard run. Now the San Francisco lead was cut to 24–14. But just as the Cowboys were feeling confident, the 49ers responded with a touchdown by Jerry Rice before halftime to extend their lead to 31–14.

In the third quarter, the Cowboys and 49ers traded touchdowns. Heading into the fourth quarter, the Cowboys trailed, 38–21. Then they mounted an impressive 89-yard drive that ended with a 10-yard touchdown pass to Irvin. The 49ers' lead was now 38–28 with 7:18 remaining.

Could Aikman pull off a miracle, Staubach-like finish? No, the San Francisco defense stiffened. On the last play of the game, the 49ers sacked Aikman. As he went down, so did the dream of a three-peat.

"After the game, I went out and sat in the car by myself crying," Jones said. "I mean, I don't think I'll ever again get that close to winning three straight Super Bowls. That's asking too much of life."

78 Thumb through *Dallas Cowboys Media Guide*

The *Dallas Cowboys' Media Guide* isn't just for the media. You can usually find a copy on eBay, and it's a great source of current and historical information on the Cowboys.

The current version is about 6-by-9 inches, and has a ring binding that easily stays open to the section that interests you. The guide begins with the Cowboys' schedule and the dates for playoff games (pretty confident, isn't it?). It's then broken down into seven sections: team officials, players, the previous season, all-time records, playoff history, overall history, and miscellaneous.

Owner Jerry Jones gets the most ink. His bio is right up front. "In one of the most dramatic eras of ownership in professional sports, Jerry Jones' stewardship of the Dallas Cowboys has brought unprecedented results and success to one of the world's most popular sports entities," it says.

The article talks about the involvement of the entire Jones family in the Cowboys organization. Jerry and Gene Jones' oldest son, Stephen, is chief operating officer. Their daughter, Charlotte, is executive vice president over brand management. Son Jerry Jr. is executive vice-president of sales and marketing.

Next, you can read about head coach Wade Phillips and the team's 14 assistant coaches, 12 scouts, and the trainer. The players' section, the longest, comes next. Each listing gives a player's height and weight, years with the team, college attended, what round he was drafted, and a year-by-year performance breakdown.

The section also includes an alphabetical listing of every player who has ever worn a Dallas Cowboys uniform, as well as his position, college attended, and years with the team. Even diehard fans would have trouble remembering some of the obscure, short-lived players on the list.

Next comes a season-by-season listing of players who received Pro Bowl honors. Hall of Fame defensive tackle Bob Lilly tops the list with 11 selections. The players' section ends with a chronology of the team's annual draft picks.

Check out the section on team records and see if you know your Cowboys history. Who is the Cowboys' all-time leading rusher? It's Emmitt Smith, who rushed for 17,162 yards from 1990 to 2002. Of course, he's also the NFL's all-time leading rusher.

Who's the team's leading receiver? Michael Irvin with 750 catches for 11,904 yards and 65 touchdowns.

The highest-rated quarterback? Roger Staubach with a QB rating of 83.4. You'll be surprised by the runner up. It isn't Troy Aikman. It's Staubach's immediate successor, Danny White. By a razor-thin margin, White had a better quarterback rating than Aikman: 81.7 to 81.6.

Who had the most interceptions? Mel Renfro with 52.

The longest kickoff return average? Renfro with an average of 26.4 yards per return.

Those are some of the statistical highlights. Hardcore fans can keep reading and discover the season-by-season offensive and defensive records, both for the team and individuals. The numbers may make your head spin after a while.

The *Dallas Cowboys Media Guide* isn't intended to be read cover to cover like a novel. It's a handy, easy-to-use reference guide bursting with information that no one could ever completely absorb and retain.

If you're a fan, it should be on your shelf.

79 Two Ugly Losses

In the course of almost 50 years, the Cowboys have had plenty of highlights, as well as lowlights. The latter includes a winless record in their first season in 1960 and a 1–15 mark in 1989.

But as far as individual games, two stand out as utter debacles: a 38–0 loss to the St. Louis Cardinals in 1970, and a 44–0 loss to the Chicago Bears in 1985. Both occurred at home.

Let's start with the first game. The Cowboys were making their initial appearance on *Monday Night Football* on November 16, 1970. The broadcast had debuted that year and become a ratings hit. The Cowboys entered the game with a 5–3 record. The Cardinals, a division rival, stood at 6–2. Dallas was led by quarterback Craig Morton, running back Duane Thomas, and receiver Bob Hayes. The Cardinals countered with quarterback Jim Hart, running back MacArthur Lane, and receiver John Gilliam.

The two teams seemed to match up well—at least until kickoff. The Cardinals began their rout with a 74-yard punt return for a touchdown. Then came a 48-yard end-around to give St. Louis a 14–0 lead in the second quarter. The Cardinals kept piling on the touchdowns, and the

Cowboys never even threatened to score. Morton was simply awful. He threw three interceptions and completed only eight of 28 passes.

"It was one of those games where the harder you try, the worse it gets," fullback Walt Garrison said.

By the fourth quarter, boos rang out in the stadium. At one point, some fans turned to the broadcast booth where former Cowboys quarterback Don Meredith was calling the game. He had retired two years earlier.

"We want Meredith!" they chanted. "We want Meredith!"

"Not a chance," he said.

Ironically, the devastating defeat marked a turning point in the season. Afterward, the Cowboys played much better and won five straight games to finish 10–4. Players credited coach Tom Landry with easing up.

"Landry realized that everyone was pushing too hard, so he relaxed everything," defensive tackle Bob Lilly said. "For the only time in my career with the Cowboys, I heard him tell everyone to just have fun. Shoot, we even started playing volleyball and touch football once a week instead of running wind sprints and sitting in the meeting room."

By winning five games in a row, the Cowboys captured the NFC East title. They won two playoff games to advance to Super Bowl V and meet the Baltimore Colts. Then their winning streak ended. The Cowboys lost, 16–13, on the game's last play.

In 1985, the Cowboys suffered another shocking shutout. The undefeated Bears, who had the league's best defense, manhandled the Cowboys. Until then, the Cowboys had shown encouraging signs. They were 7–3 when they faced the Bears, but the Bears quickly proved they were in a different league.

The 44–0 shellacking became the worst loss in Cowboys' history. The Bears knocked quarterback Danny White out early. His replacement, Gary Hogeboom, quickly threw two interceptions. At halftime, the Bears led, 24–0, and coasted to victory. Just as in 1970, the Cowboys regrouped after the shutout. They won three of their last five games to finish 10–6 and win the NFC East.

But unlike 1970, the Cowboys didn't go to the Super Bowl. The Los

Angeles Rams stunned them, 20–0, in the first playoff game to end their season. The loss was disappointing. But compared with the 44–0 setback earlier in the year, it didn't seem too bad.

80 Cleveland Collapses

In 1968, the Cowboys seemed primed to win the NFL Championship. The two previous years, they had made it to the title game, but lost narrowly to the Green Bay Packers.

The Packers, after years of dominance, were in decline. They fell to 6–7–1 in 1968 and missed the playoffs. The Cowboys, meanwhile, soared to 12–2, their best record ever. Their wins included routs of 59–13 and 45–13. The Cowboys scored the most points in the league and allowed the second-fewest.

Who could possibly beat them? In the first round of the playoffs, the Cowboys drew the Cleveland Browns, who had finished only 10–4. The Cowboys had already beaten the Browns, 28–7, in the second week of the season. Cleveland, however, turned the tables on Dallas.

Playing at home, the Browns scored first on a 38-yard field goal. The Cowboys then took the lead when linebacker Chuck Howley recovered a fumble and returned it 44 yards for a touchdown. In the second quarter, Dallas kicked a field goal and Cleveland scored a touchdown. The two teams were tied, 10–10, at halftime.

In the third quarter, the Browns returned an interception 27 yards for a touchdown, then scored another touchdown on a 35-yard run. They took a commanding 24–10 lead, and Dallas clearly was in trouble. The Cowboys managed a 47-yard field goal at the end of the third quarter to pull to within 24–13, but they could never close the gap further. In the fourth quarter, the Browns and Cowboys traded touchdowns, and the Browns triumphed, 31–20.

What happened? For starters, the Cowboys committed five turnovers, including three interceptions by quarterback Don Meredith. In the third quarter, coach Tom Landry pulled Meredith in favor of backup Craig Morton, but the Cowboys were too far behind. Landry called the upset "one of the worst days in Cowboys history."

Meredith took the loss so hard that he retired afterward. He was only 31 years old. Ironically, 1968 had been one of Meredith's best seasons. He had completed 55 percent of his passes, a career high, and tossed 21 touchdown passes. Still, Dallas fans booed him unmercifully at times, and he had grown tired of the criticism.

Landry, for one, didn't want Meredith to retire. "Going into this 10th year, Don was in the prime of his career," Landry said. "I believed he had some great years left in him."

Meredith's mind was made up. He had played his last game as a Cowboy. The next year, the Cowboys tried to rebound with Morton as their starting quarterback. Morton, a former No. 1 draft pick, had spent four years backing up Meredith and seemed ready. He had a strong arm, and his teammates believed in him. The Cowboys reeled off six straight wins to open the 1969 season. They went on to finish an outstanding 11–2–1. Rookie running back Calvin Hill, the Cowboys' No. 1 draft choice, rushed for almost 1,000 yards and was named Rookie of the Year.

Once again, the Cowboys faced Cleveland in the first playoff game. Again, Dallas was heavily favored. This time, the Cowboys got to play at home in the Cotton Bowl. But the outcome was even worse.

The Browns shut down the Cowboys' rushing and passing attacks. Hill gained only 17 yards on the ground. Morton completed only 8 of 24 passes. The Browns raced to a 24–0 lead before Dallas managed a score. The final score: Cleveland 38, Dallas 14.

Landry said he dreaded facing the media.

"I didn't know what to say," he said. "We obviously had great talent. The offensive and defensive systems worked all year. But we had lost another big one. Perhaps there was a reason, something I should have seen but overlooked. But I couldn't begin to explain it."

81 Zero Club

Coaches like hard-working, dedicated players, but every team has its share of cutups and characters. In Dallas Cowboys history, few players have been as endearingly quirky as members of the Zero Club.

You've never heard of the Zero Club? That's fine with its members, all three of them. Larry Cole, Blaine Nye, and Pat Toomay formed the club in the early 1970s to celebrate their anonymity as nameless, faceless linemen. They were all good players, but teammates remembered them more for their goofiness than their talent.

The Zero Club didn't accept new members. To express interest in joining meant you didn't embrace anonymity. Its motto: "Thou shalt not seek publicity."

Before Super Bowl VI, the Zero Club members sat together on Media Day, ready to be interviewed by inquisitive reporters.

"All the press were gathered around the big stars, Lilly and Staubach and so forth," Cole said. "No one interviewed us. It wasn't that we refused to talk. No one wanted to talk to us. After a while, I looked at the other two guys and said, 'Why are we here?'"

All three were intelligent players who didn't fit the normal jock image. Nye, for instance, graduated from Stanford. Toomay graduated from Vanderbilt. He explained the Zero Club in this way, drawing upon a literary example.

"We figured out it was like Joseph Heller wrote in *Catch-22*: There was a useful purpose in cultivating boredom," Toomay said. "It can extend your career because the more bored you are, the more time slows down, and the longer you can last."

Cole said they enjoyed their reputation as oddballs.

"We spent our time at training camp reading and doing things that typical football players might not do," he said. "We loved to argue. I would always take the business position, and Blaine would take always take the labor position, and Toomay would take the liberal college professor argument."

Nye, an offensive guard, was always quick with one-liners. Before a game against the mighty Pittsburgh Steelers, a reporter asked Nye how he would fare against All-Pro defensive tackle Joe Greene.

"His strengths match up perfectly against my weaknesses," Nye quipped.

Cole was the quietest of the three but, fittingly, became the Zero Club's spokesman. "We were all pretty self-effacing guys," he said. "I always aspired to be a crusty old fart, and I think I've done a pretty good job of that."

Despite their goofball image, all three members performed well on the field. Cole, a 16ᵗʰ-round draft choice from Hawaii, had the longest career. He played from 1968 to 1980, and was both a starter and a backup on the defensive line. He played in five Super Bowls and scored a remarkable four touchdowns during his career. Eleven years elapsed between his third and fourth touchdowns.

"Anyone can have an off-decade," Cole said afterward.

Nye, a fifth-round pick, played from 1968 to 1976. Toward the end of his career, he routinely "retired" just before training camp, then would come back as the season neared. He didn't like two-a-day practices. Landry, the ultimate disciplinarian, always welcomed Nye back because he was a solid player.

"He just never has a bad football game," Landry once said.

Toomay, a sixth-round draft choice, started a few games at defensive end and tackle but mainly served as a backup. He played from 1970 to 1974 before being traded to the Buffalo Bills. After retiring, he wrote a novel based on his experiences as a Cowboy. It was called *The Crunch*.

Peter Gent, another former Cowboy who wrote the bestselling novel *North Dallas Forty*, praised Toomay's book. He called it a "wry, witty look at life with the Dallas Cowboys during the heyday of Tom Landry and Roger Staubach."

82 Bounty Bowl

In the late 1980s, the Philadelphia Eagles replaced the Washington Redskins as the Cowboys' main rival. The Cowboys-Eagles feud grew because of the antics of Philadelphia coach Buddy Ryan. He took over the slumping Eagles in 1986, after serving as defensive coordinator for the Chicago Bears.

Ryan brought a mean, street-fighting attitude to the lowly Eagles. The Philadelphia fans and players loved Ryan, and the team adopted his take-no-prisoners approach. The Eagles, who had suffered four straight losing seasons, improved rapidly under Ryan. In his third year, 1988, Philadelphia finished 10–6 and won the NFC East.

As the Eagles improved, the Cowboys declined. In 1986, the Cowboys finished 7–9, their first losing season in 20 years. From 1986 to 1990, the Buddy Ryan era, the Eagles feasted on the struggling Cowboys. The two teams met 10 times, and the Eagles won eight.

Ryan infuriated Dallas players and coaches on October 25, 1987. Philadelphia was leading Dallas, 30–20, with only seconds left in the game. Ryan needlessly called a bomb to try to get another touchdown. The Cowboys were flagged for pass interference, and the Eagles got a first down at the Dallas 1-yard line. On the game's last play, instead of kneeling down, the Eagles ran the ball in for a touchdown to win, 37–20.

Coach Tom Landry, the consummate gentleman, was so irate he wouldn't meet Ryan at midfield after the game. Two years later, Ryan and the Cowboys mixed it up again. Jimmy Johnson, in his first year as Cowboys' coach, alleged that Ryan had put a bounty on two Dallas players, quarterback Troy Aikman and kicker Luis Zendejas.

Johnson charged that Ryan had offered his players money if they would injure either player during a Thanksgiving Day game at Texas Stadium. Allegedly, Ryan had promised $500 to any player who would knock out

Mike Ditka, shown here during a November 1969 game against the Los Angeles Rams, ended his playing career in Big D.

Aikman and $200 to get rid of Zendejas.

Zendejas, a former Eagle, said he had a tape-recorded phone conversation of a Philadelphia assistant coach telling him he was a marked man. Evidence of the tape never surfaced, but Johnson took Zendejas at his word and squawked about the alleged bounty.

During the game, Philadelphia linebacker Jessie Small injured Zendejas on a kickoff, further fueling rumors of a bounty. The Eagles trounced the Cowboys, 27–0, and Johnson fumed after the game.

"I have absolutely no respect for the way they played the game," he said. "I would have said something to Buddy, but he wouldn't stand on the field long enough. He put his big fat rear end into the dressing room."

In response, Ryan cackled.

"I've been on a diet, lost a couple of pounds," he said. "I thought I was looking good."

Johnson and the Cowboys, however, had the last laugh. After the 1990 season, Ryan was fired. He had taken the Eagles to three-straight playoffs, but they lost in the opening game each time.

In 1994, Ryan got one last chance as a head coach. He took over the Arizona Cardinals, but was canned after two seasons and a 12–20 record. Ryan never returned to the NFL. The Cowboys didn't miss him.

83 Mike Ditka

Football fans usually associate Mike Ditka with the Chicago Bears. After all, he played tight end for them for six years. He gained even more fame as head coach in 1985 by leading the Bears to victory in Super Bowl XX.

The combustible Ditka, known for his sideline tirades, has close ties to the Cowboys. He ended his 12-year playing career in Dallas in 1972, and became an assistant coach with the Cowboys the next year. Ditka remained on the Dallas staff until 1982, when he took over the Bears.

Ditka played for the Cowboys for four seasons starting in 1969. He put up modest numbers, averaging 18 catches a year and scoring five touchdowns. He brought experience, savvy and toughness to a Dallas team in search of its first championship.

He had his best year in 1971, catching 30 passes and opening holes for running backs Calvin Hill and Duane Thomas. The Cowboys compiled an 11–3 regular-season record and ran over the Miami Dolphins, 24–3, in Super Bowl VI. Ditka scored the final touchdown on a 7-yard pass from Roger Staubach.

Ditka, 6' 3" and 230 pounds, began his career as a No. 1 draft choice of the Bears in 1961. He earned Rookie of the Year honors, catching 56 passes for more than 1,000 yards and scoring 12 touchdowns. In his six seasons with the Bears, Ditka was named to the Pro Bowl five times.

In 1967, the Bears traded him to the Philadelphia Eagles. He had two sub-par seasons, largely because of injuries, before being traded to Dallas. The move rejuvenated his career. In 1969, his first season in Dallas, Ditka caught 17 passes and scored three touchdowns, the most during his Dallas career.

"To be perfectly honest, when Mike came to the Cowboys, he wasn't worth shooting," coach Tom Landry said. "He knees were bad, his legs gone. But he worked diligently with our weight coach to build his legs back up to the point where he made a valuable contribution to the Cowboys' offense for the next several years."

Fans remember Ditka's accomplishments on the field, but his teammates remember his wild man antics off the field.

"Ditka was mean," fullback Walt Garrison said. "Ditka had the foulest temper of any man I've ever met. It was so bad people used to like to get him mad just to see what he'd do because he could lose control in a slim second, and anything could happen. That was the fun of it—the element of surprise."

Garrison used to go golfing with Ditka, although Ditka didn't have the temperament for the game.

"Mike threw his club after about every shot," Garrison said. "He used to throw stuff all over. Hell, I'd just started playing golf, and I thought it was part of the game. Get mad, throw a club, cuss, beat your club on the ground, break the damn thing, throw it in the lake."

Landry also got a taste of Ditka's temper. The two occasionally played tennis when Ditka was an assistant coach.

"Even across the net from Mike you weren't safe," Landry said. "You never knew what he'd do if he missed a particularly frustrating shot. I've seen him smash his racket on the court until it looked like an aluminum pretzel, then bend it back into its approximate original shape and go on with the match.

"One day when he blew a shot," Landry said, "he angrily slung his racket at the net and missed—hitting me on the ankle and sending me hopping off the court on one foot."

Ditka always admired Landry, perhaps because Landry had the calm, measured demeanor Ditka lacked. Ditka appreciated the coaching lessons he learned from Landry.

"He was the classiest act in coaching, a great coach but a greater man," Ditka said. "I loved him for what he meant in my life and what he meant to the game."

84 Eat at Randy White's Hall of Fame Barbeque

Success never changed Randy White. Despite a Hall of Fame career, he's still the same backslapping good old boy he's always been. He's easy to find these days, unlike some former Cowboys. He owns Randy White's Hall of Fame Barbeque in Frisco, a fast-growing and affluent Dallas suburb.

If you run into White, which is distinctly possible, he'll always chat with you, sign an autograph, or pose for a photo.

Business must be good. White recently moved into a new building after many years in his original location. He may have needed more space to display all the Cowboy photos and memorabilia he's accumulated. The keepsakes are fascinating, and the food isn't just an afterthought.

At Randy White's Hall of Fame Barbeque, customers grab a tray and go through a cafeteria-style line. You can choose from a wide selection of meats: brisket, ribs, sausage, pulled pork, chicken, ham, and turkey. The brisket is so tender it falls off your fork. The sausage is lean and comes in three varieties: mild, hot, and really hot.

Go farther down the serving line and choose from potato salad, pinto beans, corn on the cob, green beans, cucumber salad, mashed potatoes, fried okra, coleslaw, or macaroni and cheese. Top off your meal with dessert: apple pie, pecan pie, peach cobbler, or banana pudding. This is real stick-to-your ribs food, the kind White himself likes.

After paying, sit down in a wooden bench in the rustic dining area. Twangy country music blares from the speakers. Photos of John Wayne and Willie Nelson adorn the rough-hewn wood walls. Most of the memorabilia displayed, however, involves the Cowboys. White has a framed, auto-graphed jersey of his, game balls he won, Cowboy team photos, and pictures of individual players.

But the real fun comes in making your way around the restaurant and spotting the unexpected. Some examples: a photo of quarterback Roger Staubach playing baseball at the Naval Academy, a photo of Hall of Fame cornerback Mel Renfro running hurdles at Oregon, and a photo of wide receiver Peter Gent (who gained fame as the author of *North Dallas Forty*) playing basketball at Michigan State.

Many ex-Cowboys have endorsed products over the years, and the restau-rant displays some of the ads. For instance, there's a framed photo of fullback Walt Garrison promoting smokeless tobacco. "A pinch is all it takes," he says in the ad.

White has plenty of photos from his playing days, which extended from 1975 to 1988. In most of them, a wild-eyed White is chasing down an opposing quarterback, such as Jim Hart of the Cardinals, Phil Simms of the Giants, or Randall Cunningham of the Eagles.

White had a very fitting nickname: the Manster. It meant he's half man, half monster. Teammate Charlie Waters came up with the nickname early in White's career and it stuck. White pays tribute to his nickname with a sand-wich called the Manster. It's two types of meat on a big bun. You can also order a Tough Man Burger, which is two half-pound hamburger patties.

If barbecue isn't your thing, White also offers fried catfish. Every Thursday night, he has all-you-can-eat catfish. On Fridays, you can sit on the patio and listen to live music. Big-screen TVs are mounted all around, tuned into football, of course.

Some star athletes struggle with life after retirement. White has not. He owns a successful restaurant, does occasional television commercials, and seems to be having a ball.

The Manster has done well for himself.

85 Craig Morton

The Cowboys made quarterback Craig Morton their No. 1 choice in the 1965 draft for good reason. He stood 6' 4", weighed 215 pounds, and had a cannon for an arm. He played little his first four seasons, primarily backing up starter Don Meredith.

When Meredith retired before the 1969 season, Morton finally had his chance to lead the team. But Morton unexpectedly felt pressure from a rookie: 27-year-old Roger Staubach. Staubach, a Heisman Trophy winner at the Naval Academy, joined the Cowboys after a four-year military commitment. The Cowboys invested only a 10th round pick in Staubach, and never knew if he would pan out. When he arrived for his first training camp, Staubach immediately impressed coaches and teammates. He had great scrambling ability and a strong, albeit erratic, arm.

Meredith warned Morton about Staubach.

"I said, 'Craig, I'm glad it's you instead of me against this guy. He's gonna get your job,'" Meredith recalled.

Coaches were intrigued by Staubach, but still saw him as a project. Morton won the starting job and had an adequate year. Meanwhile, Staubach performed adequately in his first year in 1969. In his biggest test, a playoff game against the Cleveland Browns, Morton stunk. He completed only 8 of 24 passes, and the Cleveland Browns upset Dallas, 38–14.

Heading into the 1970 season, coaches gave Staubach a harder look, but Morton still retained his job. Morton had another so-so year, and the Cowboys finished 10–4. This time, however, Morton had success in the playoffs. He led the Cowboys to two straight wins to advance to Super Bowl V against the Baltimore Colts.

In another big test, Morton failed again. He completed only 12 of 26 passes and threw a fourth-quarter interception that doomed the Cowboys. With the game tied, 13–13, and just over a minute remaining, the Cowboys had the ball. They were trying to get into position for a game-winning field goal.

Morton overthrew running back Dan Reeves in the flat, and Colts' linebacker Mike Curtis intercepted. He returned the ball 13 yards to the Dallas 28. Two short running plays set up a 32-year-field goal on the game's last play to give Baltimore a 16–13 win.

The loss shattered Morton's teammates. No one said so openly, but the team lost confidence in him after the weak performance.

In 1971, Staubach had his best chance to win the starting job. At the end of training camp, coach Tom Landry surprised everyone with his decision. He named Staubach and Morton co-starters.

After seven games, with Staubach and Morton alternating, Dallas stood at 4–3 and seemed to be going nowhere. Landry then made a bold decision, naming Staubach the lone starter. Staubach responded like a champ. He led the Cowboys to seven straight wins to finish the 1971 regular season. Under Staubach, the Cowboys won two playoff games and advanced to Super Bowl VI against the Miami Dolphins.

The Cowboys won easily, 24–3, and Staubach was named Most Valuable Player. He had completed 12 of 19 passes and threw two touchdowns.

By now, Morton's fate seemed sealed; he would return to the bench. Morton got a second chance as starter when Staubach suffered a separated shoulder in the 1972 preseason. Staubach missed most of the regular season.

Morton, starting all 14 games, had an up-and-down year. He completed 55 percent of his passes, a career best, and threw 15 touchdowns, but

Getty Images

Craig Morton played quarterback for the Cowboys from 1965 to 1974.

Morton offset them by throwing 21 interceptions.

In 1973, Staubach regained his starting job. Morton, a 10-year veteran who no longer wanted to be a backup, requested a trade. The Cowboys complied, sending him to the New York Giants in the first month of the 1974 season.

In three seasons with the Giants, Morton displayed the same inconsistency that marked his Dallas tenure. Morton threw 29 touchdown passes as a Giant from 1974 to 1976, but also an alarming 49 interceptions.

In 1977, the Giants traded Morton to the Denver Broncos. He had a solid season as starter, throwing 14 touchdowns, and was named NFL Comeback Player of the Year. More importantly, he led the Broncos to Super Bowl XII against his former team, the Cowboys.

Instead of outdoing Staubach, as he had hoped, Morton collapsed. He threw four interceptions and got yanked in the third quarter. Staubach, predictably, played well, completing 17 of 25 passes and tossing a 45-yard touchdown pass. Dallas stampeded the Broncos, 27–10.

On the biggest stage, Staubach had outshone Morton. He again demonstrated why Landry had chosen Staubach over Morton. It was a decision Landry never regretted.

86 Toni Fritsch

Like most NFL teams, the Cowboys don't keep a kicker long. After a few misses, the guy is cut. His replacement may last only a few games before he misses a key field goal and is also sent packing.

The Cowboys have had so many kickers that many have slipped into obscurity. Does anyone remember Ken Willis, Tim Seder, Shaun Suisham, Jose Cortez, or Roger Ruzek? A few kickers, however, have lodged in the collective memory of fans because of their longevity, performance (good or bad), or personality. Toni Fritsch fits into the latter category. He played from 1971 to 1973, and again in 1975.

Fritsch had been a soccer star in Austria when the Cowboys signed him. In the early 1970s, many NFL teams were changing to soccer-style, instead of head-on, kickers. The Cowboys, never wanting to miss out on a trend, dispatched some scouts to Europe to look for a soccer player who could kick field goals. They found Fritsch, an aging right winger on Austria's national team. He impressed scouts by making 29 of 30 field goals from 40 yards.

Fritsch didn't look much like a football player. He stood only about 5' 6" and carried too much weight about his middle. He began the 1971 season as a backup to veteran Mike Clark. But when Clark struggled midway through the season, coach Tom Landry switched to Fritsch. He responded well in his new sport. Fritsch made five of eight field goals, including a game-winner against the St. Louis Cardinals.

"I keeka the touchdown!" Fritsch shouted afterward.

During Fritsch's first training camp, some veterans had fun with him. They sent him out for pizza past the 11 PM curfew. The veterans, including Charlie Waters, didn't want to risk getting caught and fined for curfew violation. Fritsch sneaked out of the dorm in Thousand Oaks, California, bought the pizza and was driving back when a police officer stopped him for speeding.

Fritsch had no driver's license and didn't speak English well enough to explain where he was heading. Finally, he pointed to his Cowboys T-shirt.

"Me, Dallas Cowboys," he said, stumbling.

The cop, taking a look at Fritsch's physique, didn't buy the story and took him to the police station. Gil Brandt, player personnel director, explained the situation to police and got Fritsch released.

In 1972, his second season, Fritsch made 21 of 36 field goals. His biggest play came not on a field goal, but an onside kick. The Cowboys were playing the San Francisco 49ers in a wild-card playoff game. Dallas trailed, 28–23, with only 1:30 left in the game.

The Cowboys needed to recover an onside kick to have any chance of winning. Fritsch pulled off a perfect, albeit unusual, kick.

"Toni approached the ball on the run, stepped past it, and crazy-kicked it sideways with his trailing foot," Landry said. "The football caromed diagonally toward the 49ers on the right side of the field."

San Francisco receiver Preston Riley caught the ball and was immediately leveled. He coughed up the ball, Dallas recovered and Staubach threw a 10-yard touchdown pass to win the game.

"Had we not gotten it," Staubach said of the onside kick, "we would not have won."

In 1973, Fritsch hit 18 of 28 field goals. He missed 1974 with an injury, then returned in 1975. He made 22 of 35 field goal attempts, then was traded to San Diego after the season. By that time, Fritsch understood the difference between a field goal and a touchdown.

87 Do a Deal with Roger

Roger Staubach has been just as successful in business as he was in football. Today he heads the Staubach Co., a Dallas-based commercial real estate firm that does business worldwide. The company, formed in 1977, has a specific niche. It represents tenants, helping them find the best office, industrial, or retail space for their particular needs. The company then negotiates the lease agreement.

So if you need space for your start-up business, call Roger.

If you need larger space for your expanding business, call Roger.

If you need to negotiate a new lease, call Roger.

Of course, you probably won't get to speak to Staubach himself. You might have at one time, but today, his company employs 1,500 people in 65 offices throughout North America. The Staubach Co. has more than 3,000 clients, including Blockbuster, Office Max, T-Mobile, Time Warner Cable, and Wachovia.

Staubach has removed himself a bit from the daily operation of his company. He now carries the title of executive chairman. His thumbprint

Despite an accomplished career with the Cowboys, Leon Lett is probably best known for being infamously stripped of the ball at the goal line by Don Beebe of the Buffalo Bills during the Cowboys' 52–17 romp at Super Bowl XXVII in Pasadena.

is still all over the Staubach Co. For instance, it touts its five values: team-work, leadership, balance, respect, and integrity. You can imagine Staubach preaching those values in the locker room.

"Teams work," the company website says. "The collective efforts of varied specialists will produce extraordinary results; lone efforts do not. Fidelity to the team ethic will result in personal achievements beyond one's own capabilities."

Staubach may have written that himself. As a football player, Staubach succeeded because he worked hard, pursued goals, and never backed down from challenges. He earned the nickname Captain Comeback for his uncanny ability to lead the Cowboys to victory late in a game. Staubach, the business-man, has succeeded for many of the same reasons. He has identified opportunities, taken risks, and developed strategies to accomplish goals. In 2007, the Staubach Co. completed 7,280 transactions totaling $28 billion.

"There is really great competition out there that's as tough as playing the Redskins and Giants," Staubach said. "If you work hard, persevere, and do the right thing, there's a lot of business out there."

88 Leon Lett

Poor Leon Lett. He had not one, but two boneheaded plays during his 10-year career with the Cowboys. The one most people remember occurred in Super Bowl XXVII, the first of Dallas' three Super Bowl wins of the 1990s. The Cowboys annihilated the Buffalo Bills, 52–17. The score would have been even more lopsided if Lett, a 6' 6", 287-pound defensive tackle, hadn't sacrificed a sure touchdown by showboating.

Late in the game, Lett recovered a Buffalo fumble at the Cowboys' 35-yard line and headed for the goal line. A step or two from the end zone, Lett held the ball low to the ground in some sort of early celebration dance. Buffalo receiver Don Beebe caught up with Lett, punching the ball out of his hands and through the end zone.

The Bills took over at their own 20-yard line. If Lett had scored a touchdown, the Cowboys would have set a Super Bowl record for most points scored. As it was, the Cowboys' 52 points ranked second behind San Francisco's 55 points in Super Bowl XXIV.

Teammates and coaches could laugh about Lett's Super Bowl blunder, but no one laughed about his second gaffe less than a year later. The Cowboys were hosting the Miami Dolphins in a Thanksgiving Day game in 1993. Dallas had an unusual ice storm, and the field was covered with a slick glaze.

The Cowboys were up, 14–13, with only 15 seconds left in the game. Miami lined up for a 41-yard, game-winning field goal attempt. Defensive tackle Jimmie Jones blocked the kick, seemingly ensuring a victory.

But big Leon Lett, inexplicably, came rushing toward the ball as it bounced near the goal line. At the last second, he tried to stop but couldn't, and slid into the ball. The Dolphins recovered and kicked a 19-yard field goal on the game's last play to win, 16–14. Coach Jimmy Johnson felt sorry for Lett and went easy on him during the post-game news conference. Lett, meanwhile, hung his head in the locker room and didn't say a word. Even bloodthirsty reporters felt sorry for him and left him alone.

Days later, still unable to face the press, Lett issued a prepared statement. "I'm deeply hurt for my teammates because of the judgment error I made at the end of last week's game," he said. "In my efforts to try and help our team win, I made a poor decision. Hopefully, my performance in the future will in some way make up for my mistake."

Lett had an up-and-down career with the Cowboys from 1991 to 2000. The Cowboys drafted him in the seventh round out of Emporia State University in Kansas. He played little his rookie year because of a back injury. In his second year, 1992, he didn't start but he got a lot of playing time.

In 1993, he started six games, and he redeemed himself slightly in Super Bowl XXVIII. Lett hit Buffalo running back Thurman Thomas, forcing a fumble, early in the third quarter. Dallas safety James Washington recovered and raced 46 yards for a touchdown to tie the game, 13–13. The Cowboys seized the momentum and went on to crush the Bills, 30–13.

In 1994, Lett became a full-time starter. He recorded 68 tackles and four sacks and earned Pro Bowl honors. Big Cat, as he was called because of his extraordinary quickness, seemed destined to be a perennial Pro Bowl selection, but his career went backwards in 1995. He was suspended for four games for a drug violation, the first of three drug suspensions he would serve in his career. He played five more seasons with the Cowboys, through 2000, but never fulfilled his early promise.

In 2001, Lett signed with Denver but couldn't earn a starting spot, and retired after the season. Since then, Lett has seemingly disappeared. Even his close friends and former teammates say they rarely see him. Lett has declined all interview requests since he left football.

Fans don't remember Lett's solid play over 10 seasons. Instead, they recall his two monumental mistakes, captured forever in highlight reels.

89 Watch Cowboy Highlights

Fans can relive great moments in Cowboys history by watching a growing number of historical DVDs. They are available from several Internet sites, and most are reasonably priced. Some contain highlights from the Cowboys' five Super Bowl wins. Others focus on individual seasons or players.

One of the best sites is www.profootballdvd.com. There you'll find a couple of excellent DVDs on the Cowboys:

Dallas Cowboys: The Complete History of America's Team (1960–2003). This two-DVD set, priced at $19.95, is more than three hours in length and is a great overview of four decades of Cowboys history. The first DVD is titled *The Complete History.* It recaps the Super Bowl wins as well as some memorable regular-season games, such as the dramatic 35–34 win over the Washington Redskins in 1979. This DVD includes profiles of some great players, such as Cliff Harris, Charlie Waters, Hollywood Henderson, and Too Tall Jones. The second DVD is titled *1992 NFC*

Championship Game. It covers the Cowboys' 30–20 win over the San Francisco 49ers that let them advance to Super Bowl XXVII, the first of three Super Bowls wins of the 1990s.

Dallas Cowboys: Super Bowl Champions. This is another two-DVD set, priced at $14.95. It runs more than five hours and gives an overview of all the Super Bowl wins, starting with Super Bowl VI and ending with Super Bowl XXX. "Brace yourself for an exhilarating ride down memory lane and witness some of the best Super Bowl moments ever," the case says. The DVDs include features on stars such as Bob Lilly, Duane Thomas, Michael Irvin, and Emmitt Smith. Coach Jimmy Johnson provides commentary on the Super Bowl XXVII and Super Bowl XXVIII victories.

Another excellent site is www.nflshop.com. It has several DVDs that cover the Cowboys' Super Bowl-winning seasons. For instance, you can order individual DVDs on the 1971, 1977, and 1992 seasons. The first two cost $19.99 each, the third $26.99. The best buy is a giant four-DVD collection, more than five hours long and priced at $39.99. It reaches back to the 1966 and 1967 NFL Championship Game losses to the Green Bay Packers. It also covers the bitter 16–13 loss to the Baltimore Colts in Super Bowl V. The DVD profiles Tony Dorsett, the Cowboys' No. 1 draft pick in 1977 who helped lead Dallas to a Super Bowl win in his rookie season. The DVDs also tell the story of the Triplets, the trio of Troy Aikman, Emmitt Smith, and Michael Irvin that fueled the Cowboys' three Super Bowl wins in the 1990s.

A third website for Cowboys highlights is www.nflfilms.com. Here, you can order rare historical DVDs that are generally unavailable anywhere else. Most cost $50 each. For instance, the site has short DVDs, only 26 minutes each, on the 1966 and 1967 championship games against Green Bay. You can also order highlights of each of the Cowboys' eight Super Bowl appearances. These DVDs are short, ranging from 22 to 25 minutes. NFL Films says it doesn't sell any broadcasts of entire games. You can order short overviews of most Cowboy seasons from 1960 to the present. NFL Films also sells compilations of seasons. For instance, one DVD covers 1965 to 1969 and another 1970 to 1972. You can also buy a DVD that spans the Cowboys' first 25 seasons—1960 to 1985. The site also sells DVDs on indi-

Dat Nguyen wrestles down Philadelphia Eagles running back Duce Staley in a December 2002 game.

viduals, such as Emmitt Smith, Jimmy Johnson, and Tom Landry. If you can bear to watch it, you can buy a DVD titled *The Catch*. It covers the 1981 NFC Championship Game between Dallas and San Francisco. The 49ers won, 28–27, on a last-second touchdown catch by Dwight Clark. The heartbreaking loss kept the Cowboys out of the Super Bowl.

Two other reliable sources for Cowboys' DVDs are Amazon and eBay. A recent search of eBay revealed more than two-dozen DVDs for sale. Some are ones mentioned here, while others are different. For instance, you could buy DVDs on Roger Staubach and Bob Hayes, highlights of individual seasons and games, and some DVDs that could only be lumped under miscellaneous.

How about a documentary on the making of the 2002 Dallas Cowboys Cheerleaders' swimsuit calendar and a 1996 video titled *Dallas Cowboys Cheerleaders' Western Workout*?

It's debatable whether those qualify as official Dallas Cowboys history, but they might be worth watching anyway.

90 Dat Nguyen

Dat Nguyen broke new ground in college and as a pro. He became the first player of Vietnamese origin at Texas A&M University and in the NFL.

Nguyen, a middle linebacker, overcame enormous odds to achieve success and become a fan favorite. His parents narrowly escaped from North Vietnam in 1975, during the end of the Vietnam War. Dat was born at a refugee camp in Arkansas. Later, his parents moved to southern Texas so they could work on shrimp boats in the Gulf of Mexico.

In the eighth grade, Dat was introduced to football and immediately began to excel. He earned a scholarship to Texas A&M and became a four-year starter. He wound up setting the school record for career tackles. Nguyen stood just 5' 11" and had only average speed, but he also had an incredible knack for the ball.

"He's not big or fast, but from a production standpoint, he makes a bunch of plays," said his college coach, R.C. Slocum.

Some NFL scouts questioned whether Nguyen could make it in the pros. The Cowboys took him in the third round in 1999 and, as a rookie, he led the team in special teams tackles.

"I recall saying to myself, 'This kid is worth watching,'" safety Darren Woodson said. "He understood the game. He understood angles and pursuit. He understood how to make plays."

In his second year, Nguyen started five games. By 2001, he started every game and made 172 tackles, the second-highest season total in Cowboys' history. In 2003, Nguyen anchored a unit that finished first in the league in total defense. He made second team All-Pro. By 2005, nagging injuries began to plague Nguyen. The most serious was a neck condition that landed him on the injured reserve list toward the end of the season.

He never played again, retiring at age 30 after seven seasons. He finished his career with 665 tackles, seven interceptions, and six sacks.

Some people thought Nguyen's playing career might end when Parcells became coach in 2003. Parcell always preferred bigger linebackers.

"Almost immediately following the hiring of Parcells, people began speculating whether I was going to be traded, cut or relegated to backup duty on the bench," Nguyen wrote in his 2005 autobiography, *Dat: Tackling Life and the NFL*. "I can honestly say that none of the speculation fazed me in the least. I couldn't control my size.

"I wasn't suddenly going to grow three inches and add 20 pounds. But I knew I could play in the NFL, and I was convinced that if Coach Parcells gave me a chance, I could prove my worth to him."

He remembers meeting Parcells at Valley Ranch, the Cowboys' practice facility. Nguyen was working out on a treadmill.

"He told me we had a mutual friend in R.C. Slocum, and he made some other small talk," Nguyen wrote. "But then he point-blank asked me, 'Are you lazy?' I told him I wasn't, and he said, 'Good, because if you are lazy, you aren't going to like it around here. But if you're willing to put in the work, you'll be fine.' I got the message, and I was certainly willing to do whatever it took to prove to Parcells that I could be the exception to his 'big linebackers are better' rule."

With his breakout year in 2003, Nguyen won over Parcells.

"He's a football-playing dude," Parcells once said.

Woodson said Nguyen excelled largely because of his hard work and preparation.

"Dat was almost always the first player to arrive at Valley Ranch every morning," Woodson said. "I would typically pull into the parking lot at 6:45 AM, and his car was already parked and the engine was cool."

Nguyen was always glad to be considered a role model as the first Vietnamese-American player in the NFL. But more importantly, he wanted to be recognized by his teammates as a top-notch football player.

"I've earned their respect because of my work ethic, not my ethnicity," Nguyen wrote in his autobiography. "Inside an NFL locker room, guys care a heck of a lot more about your backbone than your background. "

91 Read About Jerry

Jerry Jones seemed to come out of nowhere when he bought the Cowboys in 1989. Cowboy fans had never heard of this oil and gas wildcatter from Arkansas. Even today, almost two decades after Jones came to town, many people still don't know much about him.

Jim Dent, a longtime Dallas sportswriter and author, paints a detailed portrait of Jones in *King of the Cowboys: The Life and Times of Jerry Jones*, a biography published in the mid-1990s. It's a good read. Dent describes Jones' modest upbringing, his high school and college football career, his up-and-down early business ventures, and the deals that made him rich.

"Jones still operates on the oil patch mentality he picked up during his early business years: roll the dice until your knuckles bleed, and never, ever do what the traditionalists would do," Dent writes. "Jones is determined to succeed on his own terms and in his own way … He doesn't mind taking a wrecking ball to tradition and traditionalists."

Jones grew up in North Little Rock, Arkansas His dad, Pat Jones, owned a fruit stand that later grew into a supermarket. Jerry put in long hours there.

"I learned to do everything in the store," Jerry says in the book. "I was up at the crack of dawn, or I'd be working until midnight on something … My dad knew I had a lot of buddies who were not that serious about working. He'd say, 'I'm going to teach you to work so that you won't mind working, and it'll be part of your personality when you grow up.'"

Starting at age 7, Jerry sold watermelons in front of the store.

"I knew Jerry had the instincts," his dad says in the book. "Even when he was a kid, he could talk to people just like he was an adult. It was a gift."

Jerry's mother, Arminta Jones, agreed. She dressed him up in a suit when he was only 9 and had him greet customers as they walked in.

"He was born to be a showman," she says. "He wanted attention from the very beginning. That was very, very clear about Jerry right from the start. He went out and worked to get it."

Jerry played football at North Little Rock High School, first as a quarter-back and then as a fullback. He wasn't particularly big or fast, but he was tough to bring down.

"He would run through a brick wall," a former assistant coach says. "He would run through it again if you didn't stop him. He would run over you and laugh at you."

Jones won a scholarship to the University of Arkansas in 1960, and eventually became a starting offensive guard, even though he was only 6' tall and weighed 190 pounds. One of the assistant coaches was Barry Switzer, whom Jones would hire three decades later to coach the Cowboys.

"Jerry was typical of the players of that age," Switzer says in *King of the Cowboys*. "Most of us made the team with hustle and try-hard. All of us white boys weren't exactly separated by our athletic skills. But we were smart enough to bust our butts."

Switzer says Jones stood out, not just on the football field.

"Jerry has always been a total extrovert," Switzer says. "A salesman. A

Jerry Jones stands in front of a nighttime artist's rendering of the Dallas Cowboys new $1 billion stadium at a news conference in December 2006.

promoter. He always had that tremendous energy level. Jerry had a drive and an authority even then that made him so well-liked."

Before leaving the University of Arkansas in 1964, Jones had earned bachelor's and master's degrees in business. He quickly began investing in real estate before getting into the oil and gas business in 1970. He had immediate success. By 1976, he sold an oil production company for a profit of $50 million.

"Jerry has never met a high-risk deal that he didn't like," a former business partner tells Dent. "He's a risk-taker, and the riskier the better. You have to be a gambler to play in this business. If you get disappointed over failure, you shouldn't be in this business."

Another partner in the 1970s says Jones "wanted to strike it rich."

"But there was one other thing," the partner says in the book. "All he could talk about was that he wanted to make enough money to buy a football team."

A decade and a half later, Jones would do just that. People who didn't know Jones were shocked that this nobody could buy the most glamorous team in football. Those who knew Jones weren't surprised in the least.

92 Shop Dallas Cowboys Online Store

Jerry Jones knows how to make money. The Cowboys' owner has proven that over and over. He never misses a bet, even on matters as small as team merchandise. No NFL team offers a wider, more diverse selection of merchandise than the Cowboys.

Visit the team's online store by going to www.dallascowboys.com and clicking on "shop." Set aside some time, maybe your entire lunch break or longer, to peruse the vast selection of essential—and unessential—stuff.

Any fan needs a team jersey, right? You don't have just a few choices, you have a few dozen. Let's say you like old players more than those of today. You can pick from players of the 1960s, such as Don Perkins or Mel Renfro;

the 1970s, Tony Dorsett, Calvin Hill, Robert Newhouse, Roger Staubach, or Rayfield Wright; or the 1990s, Troy Aikman, Michael Irvin, or Emmitt Smith. Most of the legends jerseys come in navy or white. Price: $79.99.

Among today's players, you can choose from Marion Barber, Terry Glenn, Julius Jones, Terrell Owens, Tony Romo, DeMarcus Ware, Roy Williams, or Jason Witten. Most of the jerseys come in navy or white. A few, such as the Romo and Witten jerseys, also come in a navy throwback style with white shoulders and a star. Price: $74.99.

Let's say you want an authentic jersey, exactly like the players wear, not a mere replica. Prepare to dig deep in your wallet. They go for $299.99 for Aikman, Irvin, and Smith, or $224.99 for Owens or Romo.

There's another category of jerseys, called replithentic, a middle ground between the low-end replica jerseys and the high-end authentic ones. They range from $99.99 to $124.99 and are currently available for three players: Owens, Romo, and Williams.

Finally, you can order customized jerseys with any name on the back. They cost $69.99 for a youth jersey, $89.99 for an adult replica, or $279.99 for an adult authentic.

Jerseys are only a fraction of the products offered at the online store. You can also order caps, T-shirts, and clothing such as women's swimsuits and panties; automotive items including steering wheel covers, antenna helmets, and more; household goods including blankets, aprons, toothbrushes, etc.; and novelties such as dog collars, leashes, water bowls, watches, clocks, and luggage tags.

Take a look at the caps. You can choose from almost 30 varieties in various combinations of white, blue, and pink. Some of the styles include reverse swirl, moonbeam, wing, orca, billboard slouch, basic slouch, and ladies rhinestone. Plus, the website offers visors and sock hats. The headgear ranges from $14.99 to $29.99

When it comes to shirts, you can choose from short sleeve or long sleeve in more than 50 styles. They sell for $14.99 to $29.99. Once again, Jones has the merchandise market cornered. If you register online, you can get benefits such as advance notice of discounts and new products. Jones, like any good salesman, doesn't want to make just one sale. He wants you to come back again and again.

93 Landry the Man

Tom Landry left a lasting impression on the players he coached. Eight years after his death and almost 20 years after he coached his last game, Landry remains the patriarchal symbol of the Dallas Cowboys. Most former players admire Landry for being a man of conviction who made them better football players and better people.

Landry was strict, rigid, and disciplined almost to a fault. He rarely got close to his players. Some interpreted this as aloofness. In reality, Landry had a more pragmatic reason for keeping a distance from his players. He said he didn't want a personal relationship to interfere with objectively evaluating someone.

Landry had critics. Some thought he was hypocritical. They said he openly talked about his Christian faith, yet treated players like interchangeable parts. Stars such as Duane Thomas and Thomas "Hollywood" Henderson openly clashed with Landry.

Most players looked up to him. They respected his football knowledge and admired his innovations. Players may not have liked Landry's personality, but they couldn't argue with his success. Landry lead the Cowboys to 20 straight winning seasons from 1966 to 1985—an almost unprecedented accomplishment in professional sports. His 270 wins over 29 seasons ranks him third among NFL coaches.

Many players saw Landry as a role model and mentor, even a father figure. He held tight to a set of values, such as sacrifice and teamwork. Like him or not, Landry was the same person to everyone. Some players thought Landry should loosen up and become more approachable to appeal to younger athletes. But Landry wasn't interested in changing. Many players, long after retirement, said they finally understood the football lessons and life lessons Landry tried to instill.

"You didn't have to know Tom to see he lived with integrity and honesty," middle linebacker Lee Roy Jordan said. "That example has followed me into business to this day. I think it has made a lot of us more successful."

Landry never apologized for his strict rules.

"Most successful players not only accept rules and limitations, I believe they need them," Landry wrote in his autobiography. "In fact, I believe players are free to perform at their best only when they know what the expectations are, where the limits stand. I see this as a biblical principle that also applies to life, a principle our society as a whole has forgotten: You can't enjoy true freedom without limits."

Landry had a reputation for being all business, but he also could be kind and softhearted. In 1976, for instance, Duane Thomas asked Landry for a tryout. It seemed unlikely Landry would give Thomas another chance to make the team. During his two years with the Cowboys in 1970 and 1971, Thomas openly criticized Landry and general manager Tex Schramm.

Thomas grew surly and discontent, and the Cowboys finally traded him. But by 1976, hardship had changed Thomas's demeanor. He had been cut by several teams and no longer struggled with anger. He simply wanted another chance to play football, and Landry gave him that chance.

"When he came to camp, I rooted for him," Landry wrote in his autobiography. "I think everyone did."

Thomas, however, didn't make the team. His skills and speed had eroded.

"But when Duane Thomas walked out of the Cowboys' locker room for the last time, he came by my office where we chatted cordially for a few minutes, shook hands, and wished each other well," Landry wrote. "While I still felt sad, that last parting seemed so much better than our first."

A decade earlier, Landry had broken down in the locker room after the Cowboys lost badly to the Pittsburgh Steelers. It was their fifth consecutive loss, and the 1965 season seemed to be quickly unraveling. Landry addressed the team.

"It was a very emotional speech, a motivating speech," defensive end George Andrie said. "We turned it around after that. Until then, we were just a bunch of young guys having a good time. Landry shook everybody up in Pittsburgh.… We picked it up after that, and not just a notch. I think we picked it up a number of notches."

It's fitting that Landry's name is in the Ring of Honor at Texas Stadium. It's also fitting that a nine-foot bronze statue of Landry stands outside the entrance to Texas Stadium. He'll always remain a towering figure over the Cowboys organization.

"I find myself today asking, 'What would Coach Landry do?'" quarterback Danny White said.

94 Attend Dallas Desperados Game

Cowboys tickets have gotten so expensive, the average Joe can no longer afford to go to games. Ticket prices will rise even more when the Cowboys move to their new $1 billion stadium in 2009.

So how can the masses see professional football in person? Go see Dallas' other pro team: the Dallas Desperados. Tickets for their games range from only $12 to $48. Season ticket packages start at only $90—less than you'd probably pay for a single Cowboys ticket.

Okay, we're not exactly talking apples to apples here. The Desperados play indoors on a 50-yard field, not outside on a 100-yard field. The talent level in the Arena Football League can't compare to the talent in the National Football League.

But the Desperados still play pro football nonetheless. Plus, they're owned by the Cowboys. The Desperados' president and general manager is Jerry Jones Jr., son of the Big Man himself. The Desperados aren't exactly a feeder team for the Cowboys, but occasionally a player will go from one roster to the other.

For instance, Clint Stoerner was a backup quarterback for the Cowboys from 2000 to 2003. Later, he was the Desperados' starting quarterback in 2005. In addition, defensive end Shante Carver, a bust as the Cowboys' No. 1 draft pick in 1994, wound up with the Desperados from 2002 to 2004.

Fans get plenty of excitement for their buck at a Desperados game. Indoor football is much more wide open and higher scoring than the traditional game. Normally, the winning team scores 50 or more points. Occasionally, both teams combine for more than 100 points. Punting isn't allowed. Teams must go for a first on fourth down.

Running backs don't get much work in the arena league. Teams usually run the ball only a handful of times a game. Defenses expect the pass, but offenses still find ways to get receivers open.

The Desperados currently have one of the all-time great arena quarterbacks in Clint Dolezel, a graduate of East Texas State University. He joined the team in 2006 as a 10-year veteran and ranked second in completions and fourth in passing yardage in AFL history.

In Dallas, Dolezel isn't nearly as big a deal as Cowboys' quarterback Tony Romo. And Dolezel certainly doesn't make Romo-type money. Doezel's salary barely reaches six figures. Romo signed a six-year, $67.5 million contract last year.

But Dolezel isn't complaining. In 2007, he threw his 800th touchdown pass as a pro.

That's a record Tony Romo won't ever match.

95 A Hall of Famer You Don't Know

Most of the Cowboys in the Pro Football Hall of Fame are household names: Troy Aikman, Michael Irvin, Tony Dorsett, Roger Staubach, Randy White, and others. But there's another Cowboy in the Hall who rarely comes to mind. He spent only one of his 12 seasons with Dallas.

His name is Tommy McDonald. He was a 5' 9", 178-pound receiver who weaved his way through secondaries and used his speed to break long runs. McDonald, an All American at Oklahoma, began his career in 1957 with the Philadelphia Eagles. As a rookie, he logged little playing time and caught only nine passes.

In his second year, 1958, McDonald grabbed 29 passes and scored nine touchdowns. In his third year, McDonald caught 47 passes and scored 10 touchdowns. He also made his first Pro Bowl and established himself as one of the league's most dangerous offensive threats.

McDonald played seven seasons in Philadelphia, ending in 1963. During that time, he caught 287 passes for 5,499 yards and scored a remarkable 66 touchdowns. He was truly a game-breaker. He scored touchdowns of 91, 75, 71, 66, 64, 61, and 60 yards.

In 1964, the Cowboys traded three players for McDonald. Dallas needed a receiver, and McDonald was glad to arrive with a young team on the rise. However, he never became a major part of the offense. He averaged only 13.3 yards per catch, the lowest of his career, and scored only two touchdowns, also the lowest. The Cowboys threw more to the other starting receiver, Frank Clarke, who made All-Pro in 1964.

"One of the things I suppose I'll always regret about my athletic career is the fact that I didn't perform as well for Dallas as I felt I should," McDonald said.

After the season, he asked to be traded, and the Cowboys accommodated. They sent him to the Los Angeles Rams, where he regained his top form. He caught 67 passes for 1,036 yards and scored nine touchdowns in 1965. He had another strong season in 1966.

After two years in L.A., McDonald was traded to the Atlanta Falcons. He played only one season, and his receiving numbers dropped to the lowest of his career. He played his final season, 1968, with the Cleveland Browns. He clearly was well past his prime. McDonald caught only seven passes and scored one touchdown.

However, his career numbers are stellar, even by today's standards. In 12 seasons, he caught 495 passes for 8,410 yards and scored 84 touchdowns. He made the Pro Bowl six times. The highlights of his career include winning the NFL Championship in 1960 with the Eagles and leading the league in receiving yards and in touchdowns in 1961.

McDonald was elected to the Hall of Fame in 1998, three decades after he retired. He laughs that he's the shortest player ever inducted.

"All my life, all I ever heard was, 'You're too small. You'll only get hurt,'" he said. "Well, sir, I made that my fuel. That was what fed my engine. I'd show them."

Despite his size, McDonald was extremely durable. In his first 11 seasons, he missed only three games because of injury. He'd take big hits from players seemingly twice his size and immediately jump back up.

"I made that my signature, that bouncing up, just to let them know they hadn't hurt me, that they weren't going to intimidate me," McDonald said.

He never wore a facemask, becoming the league's last holdout.

"In those days, it was just a single bar, not that much protection, really, and it really distracted me," he said. "I was always blessed with good reflexes. I could see the hit coming, and I'd turn my head. They'd get the helmet but not me."

Vince Lombardi, the legendary coach of the Green Bay Packers, once made a ringing endorsement of McDonald. It speaks volumes about his attitude as a player.

"You give me 11 Tommy McDonalds," the coach said, "and I'd win the championship every year."

96 Murder Mystery

Colin Ridgway played only one year for the Cowboys, and he didn't do much to distinguish himself. He was a punter who had a mediocre 39-yard average before being cut.

Yet, Ridgway's name pops up in the local media every few years. The reason isn't related to football. Ridgway was murdered in his upscale Dallas home in 1993, and the crime has never been solved. The slaying has confounded local police and angered Ridgway's friends.

Three years after the slaying, police arrested a man and alleged a murder-for-hire plot, but he was never convicted. They also suspected his wife, but she was never convicted either.

Ridgway, 56, was shot seven times from close range after he entered his home about 10:30 PM He and his wife, Joan, had eaten dinner together and returned home in separate cars. She found Colin lying in a pool of blood and called 911. No weapon was found, and there was no sign of forced entry. Some drawers had been ransacked.

Prosecutors have long maintained that Joan arranged a murder-for-hire to collect $500,000 in life insurance. They say Ken Bicking Jr., the son of a friend of hers, committed the slaying in exchange for $5,000. The man became a suspect when his estranged wife said the man confessed to her.

Bicking was indicted for murder, and the case was only days from trial when a judge dismissed the charge. He ruled that Bicking's alleged confession was inadmissible because of a guarantee of confidentiality between spouses.

Attention focused on Joan Ridgway because she and Colin had had a tumultuous 16-year marriage. They separated twice and filed for divorce before getting back together. Her two adult daughters from a previous marriage sued their mother over the life insurance policy on Colin, their stepfather. The daughters believed their mother was involved in his death and shouldn't receive the insurance proceeds.

"There's not a doubt in my mind," said Erinn Bryan, the younger daughter.

Joan, an artist, remained in Dallas after Colin's death. But many of her friends cut her off, and she lived largely in seclusion. She has made few comments to police or the press since he died. During a grand jury investigation in 1994, she refused to answer questioning, invoking her Fifth Amendment rights against self-incrimination.

An FBI investigation concluded that Ridgway knew his killer.

"The murder specialists say that this was not an impulsive act committed during the commission of a burglary, but rather a professional crime committed by an organized offender, who then staged the crime scene to look like a burglary," police said a year after the murder.

Ridgway was a native of Australia who took a circuitous route to the Dallas Cowboys. He competed in the 1956 and 1960 Olympics as a high jumper for his native Australia. He also played rugby in the country. He moved to the United States in the early 1960s to attend college. After graduating in 1965, he signed with the Cowboys as a punter.

Ridgway had a strong leg and once punted a ball 75 yards. But he suffered from inconsistency. He was cut after an exhibition game in San Francisco. With the wind blowing about 50 miles per hour, Ridgway kicked a ball that went straight up and came straight down at the line of scrimmage.

Years later, he laughed about the incident.

"Let's face it," he said, "it's what people remember me for."

Now, however, he's remembered as the victim of a brutal murder—one that may never be solved.

97 Visit Don Meredith Museum

Don Meredith grew up in the little town of Mount Vernon, Texas, about 100 miles northeast of Dallas. He never forgot his roots, and the townspeople never forgot Don.

"He's our claim to fame," said Mayor J.D. Baumgardner.

Meredith, the first star quarterback of the Cowboys, is still a hero in his hometown. The modest, one-story house where he lived has a sign out front that says, "Don Meredith's Boyhood Home."

In 2006, local leaders decided to honor Meredith with an exhibit of his life. They wrote to Meredith, who now lives in Santa Fe, New Mexico, and asked if he'd donate some of his memorabilia. They expected a few boxes. Instead, Meredith sent five large shipments—everything from high school jerseys to college photos to Cowboys game balls.

"There were vanloads and vanloads and vanloads," said Baumgardner, who also is the museum director. "We had it all cataloged and inventoried."

The Don Meredith Exhibit at the Old Depot Museum is housed in a single room, about 30 feet by 30 feet. The Franklin County Historical Association hired a firm to organize the mementos, and the results are impressive. The museum has three large showcases. One highlights his early childhood and his days as star quarterback of the Mount Vernon Tigers. The second is devoted to his college career at Southern Methodist University and his professional career with the Cowboys. The final showcase commemorates his broadcasting career with *Monday Night Football*.

Each exhibit chronicles a separate chapter in Meredith's life. Taken as a whole, they demonstrate what a full and varied life Meredith has enjoyed.

Dandy Don came to Mount Vernon for the museum opening in fall 2006, and he was treated like a dignitary. Hundreds of people lined up on the street to get his autograph. Meredith patiently signed each one, posed for photos, and shared stories.

The event coincided with Meredith's 50th high school reunion, and he donned his old maroon-and-white letter jacket, which still fits nicely. Meredith was class president and named Most Talented.

"Everybody loved Don," Baumgardner said.

The museum may be small, no bigger than some bedrooms, but a visitor could spend hours there. There are films of his high school games, radio broadcasts of his college games, and a 20–minute interview with Meredith done by a Dallas TV station a few years ago.

Meredith's humor and corniness shine through brightly. He recalls his days as a broadcaster, paired with the pompous and sometimes irritating Howard Cosell. Meredith was part of the *Monday Night Football* team from its first year in 1970 to 1973, and then again from 1977 to 1984.

"They pretty much said, 'Don, be yourself,'" Meredith recalled in the interview. "It worked out all right. Howard made my job easy. If I sat there long enough, he'd say something stupid. He had a sense of taking himself too seriously. I knew no one else did."

The interview has poignant moments, too. Meredith talks about retiring from the Cowboys in 1968 after nine seasons. He was only 31 years old. A year later, he said, he regretted his decision and inquired about making a comeback. But the team didn't encourage him.

"One of the things that surprised me was there was so little interest in me coming back," he said.

Meredith provided so many mementos, more than 600, that museum organizers couldn't fit them all into the exhibit space. So the displays will continuously rotate. Every time someone visits, they may see something new.

More than 3,000 people visit the Don Meredith Exhibit annually, Baumgardner said. They come from all over the United States and even from other countries. People sign a guest register and often write their favorite memory of Meredith.

"It's just amazing," Baumgardner said. "The stories you can't imagine. Everybody has a story to tell about why they think so much of Don."

Admission to the museum is free, although donations are suggested. It's open Tuesday through Saturday from 10 AM to 4 PM The museum phone number is (903) 537–7012.

98 Larry Allen

There's little debate about the greatest offensive tackle in Dallas Cowboys history. It's Larry Allen. He's also one of the greatest linemen in NFL history.

Allen played for the Cowboys from 1994 to 2005. He had enormous size, strength, and quickness. Allen, 6' 3" and 325 pounds, opened countless holes for Emmitt Smith in his quest to become the NFL's all-time leading rusher.

"No one was more explosive, had the strength or could run as well to be such a big man," said Larry Lacewell, the Cowboys' former scouting director.

Allen barely missed playing on the Cowboys' two Super Bowl teams in 1992 and 1993. But he was along for the third win in 1995. Allen manhandled the Pittsburgh Steelers' defensive line as Dallas rolled to a 27–17 win in Super Bowl XXX.

The Cowboys drafted Allen in the second round in 1994 out of tiny Sonoma State University near San Francisco. He immediately contributed, starting several games for injured tackles Mark Tuinei and Erik Williams. In his second season, Allen became a starter at guard and earned Pro Bowl honors.

Larry Allen, shown here during an October 2005 game, is the greatest offensive lineman in Dallas Cowboys history.

Toward the end of the season, Allen suffered a sprained ankle. He wasn't 100 percent when the Cowboys met the 49ers in the 1994 NFC Championship Game. San Francisco jumped out to an early 21–0 lead before the Cowboys pulled closer, eventually losing, 38–28.

Teammates admired Allen for playing, despite having a weak, painful ankle. If he'd been healthy, the game's outcome might have been different, they said.

"I don't think anyone realizes the job Larry did for us," quarterback Troy Aikman said.

The soft-spoken Allen improved each year. He astounded teammates with his strength, bench pressing more than 500 pounds. After making his first Pro Bowl in 1995, Allen repeated for six straight seasons. He missed out in 2002 because of a nagging ankle sprain that limited him to only five games.

In 2003, Allen came back strong, starting all 16 games and earning Pro Bowl honors again. In 2004 and 2005, he returned to the Pro Bowl. He had one of his finest seasons in 2005, his last in Dallas. Allen played every offensive snap.

After the season, Allen was due a $2 million signing bonus, and the Cowboys chose not to re-sign him. He was the last member of the Super Bowl XXX team still active. Several teams, including Miami, Detroit, and Oakland, pursued him. He eventually signed a two-year contract with San Francisco. The 49ers were in a rebuilding mode when they signed Allen, but coach Mike Nolan said Allen could be a mentor to young linemen.

"I think Larry has got a mindset that every offensive lineman should have," Nolan said.

Allen proved his worth, helping running back Frank Gore gain a club record 1,695 yards rushing. After the 2007 season, Allen said he was considering retirement. Whenever he retires, he'll eventually be a first-ballot Hall of Fame selection.

He's already achieved legendary status with the Cowboys. Allen's 10 Pro Bowl selections rank behind only Bob Lilly, who made 11 Pro Bowls at defensive tackle.

"Larry has been the best in pro football for a long time," Cowboys owner Jerry Jones said when he released Allen in 1995. "His ability and performance set a standard for excellence at his position in the NFL for many years, and we are grateful for his contributions to the Dallas Cowboys."

99 Marion Barber

Marion Barber performs like a starter, even though he's a backup. In 2007, he rushed for 975 yards and scored 10 touchdowns, despite coming off the bench. He became one of the few backups ever chosen to the Pro Bowl.

Barber racked up such impressive numbers by getting into games early and often. Fans sometimes wondered why coach Wade Phillips didn't name Barber the starter over Julius Jones. Jones finished with 588 yards rushing.

Phillips never gave a clear answer. Jones had a better season in 2006, so he earned the right to keep his starting job. But Barber seemed to get better each week in 2007. He and Jones are dramatically different runners. Jones, a 2004 pick out of Notre Dame, is faster and more of a north-south runner. Jones sees an opening and bolts through it toward the goal line. But if there's not a clear hole, he often gets stopped at the line.

Barber, on the other hand, rarely runs where the play is designed to go. He's a master of improvisation with the football. If he doesn't see a hole when he takes the handoff, he'll bounce outside and start juking and weaving up the field. Defenders can't get a clean shot at him.

Barber, a 2005 draft choice from Minnesota, is stockier and more powerful than Jones. Barber doesn't glide up the field. He careens off tacklers like a pinball, his head bobbing, his long dreadlocks flapping from underneath his helmet.

Barber has an incredible knack for scoring touchdowns near the goal line. If the Cowboys needed two or three yards to get into the end zone, Barber usually got the call in 2007. Barber became a fan favorite. The nickname Marion the Barbarian stuck, and Barber T-shirts became big sellers.

The one-two punch of Jones and Barber helped Dallas compile its outstanding 13–3 record in 2007. In the opening playoff game against the New York Giants, however, coach Wade Phillips decided to start Barber. On paper, the change made sense. Barber clearly had become the more effective back.

But what comes to mind is that old saying, "If it ain't broke, don't fix it." Heading into the playoffs, most coaches won't make a major lineup change. In the first half against the Giants, Phillips looked like a genius. Barber was on fire. He rushed for 101 yards and the Giants couldn't stop him.

But in the second half, the Giants shut down Barber, limiting him to only 28 yards. The Giants also pressured quarterback Tony Romo, forcing him to make bad throws. The Cowboys' offense ground to a halt, and the Giants pulled off a shocking 21–17 upset.

With the year over, fans wondered how Phillips would handle the two backs in the 2008 season.

Many assumed Barber would be the starter because he got the nod in the New York playoff game. On the other hand, the Giants neutralized Barber in the second half. Maybe Phillips would second-guess himself and go back to starting Jones, with Barber coming in later and getting most of the carries.

The drama never materialized. In early March, three months after the 2007 season ended, Jones signed a lucrative four-year contract with the Seattle Seahawks. Now Barber has the job all to himself.

The Cowboys may regret letting Jones get away. Sure, his rushing numbers had slipped dramatically—from 1,084 yards in 2006 to only 588 in 2007. But he and Barber complemented one another and kept defenses guessing with their different running styles. In the long grind of an NFL season, it's critical to have two solid running backs.

Maybe Barber will blossom into a full-fledged superstar now that he'll get more carries and be the undisputed starter. Or he could suffer from overuse and be prone to injuries.

Time will tell.

100 Crazy Ray

Everybody loved Crazy Ray. Some NFL teams have cheerleaders, some have mascots. But no team has had anyone quite like Crazy Ray.

He was a fun-loving guy who wore a garish blue-and-white western outfit, complete with chaps and a 10–gallon hat. He patrolled the sidelines for more than 40 years, leading cheers and taunting opponents. He first appeared at Cowboy games in the 1960s at the Cotton Bowl. Crazy Ray made the move with the Cowboys to Texas Stadium in 1971.

His act generally remained the same. He whistled loudly. He made animals out of balloons. He "rode" a broomstick horse. He wiped his sweaty brow with an opponents' pennant. He whooped, hollered, and he fired imaginary shots with his six-shooters.

Dallas Cowboy fans are notoriously highbrow, but even the hoity-toity loved Crazy Ray. He was the anti-Cowboy fan: loud, obnoxious, and unafraid to be silly. Cowboy management tolerated Crazy Ray in the early years but weren't sure what to make of him. As time passed Crazy Ray's popularity grew, and officials knew better than to run him off. The team never paid him, but it gave him a special stadium parking place and access to the sidelines.

Crazy Ray's real name was Wilford Jones. Jones, a Korean War veteran, moved to Dallas from East Texas in 1953 to shine shoes for a living. He was 22 years old. Soon, he began entertaining children outside the downtown barbershops where he worked. He performed magic tricks, whistled, and made balloon animals.

In the early 1960s, he began selling seat cushions and souvenirs at Cowboys games. But he did more than sell, he entertained fans with his boisterous antics. Eventually, team officials asked him to stop selling items and focus on being an entertainer. Jones had found his calling as Crazy Ray.

"The whole thing turned out so much bigger than I ever expected," he said in a 1981 interview. "I never want to do anything else."

His fame spread, and he began making personal appearances in full Crazy Ray regalia. He even had a few parts in commercials and movies. He loved the attention and people loved him.

In the late 1980s, however, Crazy Ray's health began to deteriorate. He eventually underwent five heart bypass operations, suffered four strokes, and had a leg amputated. Still, he performed at many games, even while wearing a prosthesis. Eventually, he became confined to a wheelchair. Finally, glaucoma blinded him.

Jones and his wife of more than 50 years, Mattie, sank deep into debt. Their house fell into disrepair, and the utilities were turned off. A neighbor set up a website to raise money for the Joneses and renovate their home.

On the website, longtime fans shared their memories of Crazy Ray.

"I first met Ray 37 years ago at the Cotton Bowl during a Packer-Cowboy game," one man wrote. "He is and always will be, Crazy Ray, Mr. Cowboy. God bless you, Ray."

Another person said, "Crazy Ray has been an important figure of the Dallas Cowboys since I was a little boy. He has been as important to Cowboy fans as the blue star!"

Crazy Ray died in March 2007 while in hospice care at age 76. A public memorial service was held at Texas Stadium.

"Ray was the most dedicated, entertaining and passionate of Cowboys fans," team owner Jerry Jones said. "He touched thousands of lives and generations of football fans. He will remain an important part of this team's heritage and family for as long as fans go to Cowboys games and feel his spirit."

Some fans called for Jones to induct Crazy Ray into the Ring of Honor, alongside such legendary players as Roger Staubach, Bob Lilly, and Tony Dorsett.

No doubt, Crazy Ray would fit right in.

Bibliography

Allsports.com

Associated Press

Burton, Alan. *Dallas Cowboys Quips & Quotes*. Abilene, TX: State House Press, 2006.

Dallas Cowboys Media Guide, 2006.

Dallascowboys.com.

Dent, Jim. *King of the Cowboys: The Life and Times of Jerry Jones*. Holbrook, MA: Adams Media Corp., 1995.

Donovan, Jim, Ken Sims, and Frank Coffey. *The Dallas Cowboys Encyclopedia*. Secaucus, NJ: Carol Publishing Group, 1996.

Dorsett, Tony, and Harvey Frommer. *Running Tough: Memoirs of a Football Maverick*. New York: Doubleday, 1989.

Eisenberg, John. *Cotton Bowl Days*. **New York:** Simon & Schuster, 1997.

Espn.com

Fisher, Mike, and Richie Witt. *The 'Boys are Back*. Fort Worth, Texas: The Summit Group, 1993.

Garrison, Walt, and Mark Stallard. *Then Landry Said to Staubach..." The Best Dallas Cowboys Stories Ever Told*. Chicago, IL: Triumph Books, 2007.

Golenbock, Peter. *Cowboys Have Always Been My Heroes*. New York: Warner Books, 1997.

Gruver, Ed. *The Ice Bowl*. Ithaca, NY: McBooks Press, 1998.

Guinn, Jeff. *Dallas Cowboys: The Authorized Pictorial History*. Arlington, TX: Summit Publishing Group, 1996.

Harris, Cliff, and Charlie Waters. *Tales From the Dallas Cowboys*. Champaign, IL: Sports Publishing LLC, 2006.

Holmes, Michael. *Mamas, Don't Let Your Cowboys Grow Up to be Babies.* Toronto: ECW Press, 1998.

Jensen, Brian. *Where Have All Our Cowboys Gone?* New York: Cooper Square Press, 2001.

Johnson, Jimmy and Ed Hinton. *Turning the Thing Around: Pulling America's Team Out of the Dumps—And Myself Out of the Doghouse.* New York: Hyperion, 1993.

Johnston, Daryl. *Watching Football: Discovering the Game Within the Game.* Guilford, CT: Globe Pequot Press, 2005.

Kaski Briggs, Jennifer. *The Book of Landry.* Nashville, TN: TowleHouse Publishing Company, 2000.

Klein, Dave. *Tom and the Boys.* New York: Zebra Books, 1990.

Landry, Tom and Gregg Lewis. *Tom Landry: An Autobiography.* New York: HarperCollins Publishers, 1990.

Luksa, Frank. *Cowboys Essential.* Chicago: Triumph Books, 2006.

Lyon, Bill. *When the Clock Runs Out: 20 NFL Greats Share Their Stories Of Hardship and Triumph.* Chicago, IL: Triumph Books, 1999.

Martin, Harvey. *Texas Thunder: My Eleven Years with the Dallas Cowboys.* New York: Rawson Associates, 1986.

Monk, Cody. *Legends of the Dallas Cowboys.* Champaign, IL: Sports Publishing LLC, 2004.

NFL.com

NFLplayers.com

Nguyen, Dat. *Dat: Tackling Life and the NFL.* College Station, Texas: Texas A&M University Press, 2005.

Official Dallas Cowboys Bluebook, 1983.

Official Dallas Cowboys Bluebook, 1986.

Profootballhof.com.

Pro-football-reference.com

St. Angelo, Ron and Norm Hitzges. *The Greatest Team Ever: The Dallas Cowboys Dynasty of the 1990s*. Nashville: Thomas Nelson, 2007.

St. John, Bob. *Tex! The Man Who Built the Dallas Cowboys*. Englewood Cliffs, NJ: Prentice Hall, 1988.

St. John, Bob. *Landry: The Legend and the Legacy*. Nashville: Word Publishing, 2000.

Sham, Brad. *Stadium Stories: Dallas Cowboys*. Guilford, CT: Globe Pequot Press, 2003.

Shropshire, Mike. *The Ice Bowl*. New York: Donald I. Fine Books, 1997.

Smith, Emmitt. *The Emmitt Zone*. New York: Crown Publishers, 1994.

Staubach, Roger, Sam Blair, and Bob St. John. *First Down, Lifetime to Go*. Waco, TX: Word Books, 1974.

Staubach, Roger and Frank Luksa. *Time Enough to Win*. Waco, TX: Word Books, 1980.

Stowers, Carlton. *Cowboys Chronicles*. Austin, TX: Eakin Press, 1984.

Stowers, Carlton. *Dallas Cowboys: The First Twenty-Five Years*. Dallas: Taylor Publishing Company, 1984.

Stowers, Carlton. *Journey to Triumph*. Dallas: Taylor Publishing Company, 1982.

Taylor, Jean-Jacques. *Game of My Life: Dallas Cowboys*. Champaign, IL: Sports Publishing LLC, 2006.

Towle, Mike. *Roger Staubach: Captain America*. Nashville: Cumberland House Publishing Company, 2002.

Whittingham, Richard. *The Dallas Cowboys: An Illustrated History*. New York: Harper & Row, 1981.